D0099286

The Vixen Diaries

also by **Karrine Steffans**
Confessions of a Video Vixen

The Vixen Diaries

KARRINE STEFFANS

NEW YORK   GRAND CENTRAL
PUBLISHING   BOSTON

Grand Central Publishing
Hachette Book Group USA
237 Park Avenue
New York, NY 10017

Printed in the United States of America

Grand Central Publishing is a division of Hachette Book Group USA, Inc.
The Grand Central Publishing name and logo is a trademark of
Hachette Book Group USA, Inc.

ISBN-13: 978-0-446-58226-1

To Naiim and to Bill
Loving you makes it all possible

Contents

Contents
viii

Iconoclast

If video killed the radio star, then *Video Vixen* killed the entertainment industry, gutted it, and showed its insides to the world. On June 28, 2005, they broke the seal on my first book, *Confessions of a Video Vixen*. At that moment, the planets shifted and realigned, and the world as I knew it disappeared. With passages detailing my troubled upbringing and my adventures as a courtesan to many of the hip-hop elite, actors, and sports heroes, I did the one thing forbidden in my culture and demographic: I told.

It's not as if this hadn't been done before. One of the most infamous examples of sleep-and-tell was Pamela Des Barres, author of *I'm with the Band*. Publishing in 1987, Pamela salaciously described her life as a groupie. She slept with many of the most prominent rock stars of our day, including Mick Jagger, Jimmy Page, Keith Moon and Jim Morrison, while she was submerged in the 1960s Hollywood drug and club scene.

Still, my little book managed to cause surprising shock waves through "polite" society with reverberations of "How dare she!" "Who does she think she is?" and, my personal favorite, "A real woman would have kept her mouth shut." For reasons that I am still discovering, it has been difficult for some within the black culture to digest my best-selling memoir, though it is deeply rooted in that culture. In general, I have found that many members of the black community have been angered by my revelations of the truth and by my destruction of their fantasies about celebrity icons.

I have found the most inspiration and purpose in the responses of my female counterparts. Part of my reason for penning such a candid account of my life was the concept that though my exploits are not experiences of the majority, they are, sadly, more common than admitted, and in need of addressing. Although many readers were shocked by the stories I revealed, they would be astonished to know what I left out. For example, I did not include my affair with one of the most famous men ever to reach the Oscar-winning heights of the American stage and screen. I left it out because he is too powerful a figure to rub the wrong way, and in a town where relationships are everything, it's important—even vital—that I not burn any bridges. For that reason, I will refer to him as the Icon.

The Icon and I met during the winter of 2000 at the home of *Soul Food* director George Tillman, and we remained casual acquaintances for some time afterward. Tillman's party was an intimate gathering of mostly young women, all Hollywood hopefuls. I was invited by a music video casting director and, in my naïveté, hadn't realized until I arrived that this party was, essentially, a casting for the role of the Icon's bed partner. Directors and producers will, from time to time, try to impress and lure an actor by offering up delectable female party favors.

When I walked in and saw the living room of the hilltop home flooded with scantily clad video girls and B actresses, I got the feeling I didn't belong there. At the time, I just wasn't confident enough in myself to think I would attract someone as powerful as the Icon, and besides, I wasn't dressed for the occasion. It was cold out, and I dressed for the weather, wearing a body-hugging Baby Phat denim suit with boots—every inch of my body was covered.

I was also having trouble with my contact lenses and found myself spending a lot of time in the bathroom, trying to clean them and put them back in. It was during one of these trips to the bathroom that I heard a bit of commotion in the living room, followed by the Icon's unmistakable voice. I decided to leave my contacts out and to put on my glasses, which were in my car, and slowly slip out of the party. I opened the door quietly and eased out of the bathroom, only to find myself face to face with the Icon himself. My vision was blurry and my eyes were watery, but even through the mist I could see his handsome face light up. I was instantly smitten, flattered, and almost speechless.

"Well, hello there," he said.

"Hello there, yourself."

"Why haven't I seen you tonight?"

"Oh, ummm, I was in the bathroom taking out my lenses. They're giving me a lot of trouble, so I'm actually on my way out."

"Well, I was just leaving, so let me walk you out."

I was surprised he hadn't found anyone else to get to know while at the party. On the other hand, he hadn't been there very long—about thirty minutes at the most—before making his exit. I was even more surprised that he would find me—the most fully dressed woman at the party, with blurry, watery eyes—even remotely attractive.

A few days after exchanging numbers, I was invited to his home in Beverly Hills late at night. As I drove down one of the canyons searching for his house, I was startled by the sight of the Icon standing outside in his driveway wearing pajamas, bed slippers, and a bathrobe. It was amazing to see this almost legendary figure of film and American culture standing in his driveway at three in the morning, weathering the cold just to signal me into his courtyard.

The entire experience felt like a dream. I was so young at the time, and Hollywood, its pleasures, and its dangers, were still very new to me. Nevertheless, I was under no illusions about why I was there. You show up at a man's house at three in the morning and there's no party going on, you sort of know what to expect. All I saw was an opportunity to be with one of the most powerful men in Hollywood, and the opportunity just to say that I did it—and by *it,* I mean have sex with the Icon.

Even though I expected the sex, the experience was more than I bargained for. Just four minutes after I entered his home, the Icon was examining my fingernails. "Did you just have your nails done?" he inquired.

"Yeah, today actually. Why?"

"I love being scratched with freshly sharpened nails. Here, scratch my back for me."

He removed his robe and pajama shirt and turned his back to me as we stood in the doorway of his bedroom. At first, I didn't think there was anything strange about a man wanting his back scratched—not until his next request: "Harder."

I pressed a little harder, thinking his back must be really itchy. "Like this?"

"No, harder. Don't be afraid, you won't hurt me. It's okay if you leave marks. Come on, harder."

It all still felt like a dream, and as I stood in his palatial home in the middle of the night, I didn't know how to say no to this super megastar. I scratched harder and harder still, until long, bright red marks formed on his back. I was on the verge of drawing blood. I cringed in fear of hurting him, but he moaned and groaned with pleasure. I was disgusted; my attraction to him quickly waned. I felt nauseated, and that feeling was only magnified by what happened next.

We began to kiss awkwardly and fumbled out of our clothes and into the bed. All the while, I was planning my escape. I wanted to tell this A-list name-above-the-title movie star that I had wasted his time, that I no longer wanted to be around him. I never got the chance. The next thing I knew, he was on all fours and naked on the bed. I don't have a strong enough stomach to describe what happened in the hours that followed except to say that, for him, it was all anal.

Whenever I have told someone that I used to see the Icon, their eyes get big and they get excited for me, as if I had accomplished a huge, worthy feat by having sex with him. There are times when meeting the man of your dreams is all you expect it to be, but those times are rare. It's more likely that you'll find yourself disappointed and even disgusted after it's over. So many, including me, spend our lives trying either to become an icon or to get next to one. Truth be told, neither scenario is usually what you'd expect, and there are days when I wish I could turn back the hands of time and change it all. The irony is, I have become an icon by sleeping with many of them. Something about that gives me an uncomfortable feeling, and not because of my sexual roster but because of the weight that society places on the celebrities on it. For *this* I am iconic? Jeez.

Viva La Vixen!

After I wrote *Confessions,* I believed that once I became successful, life would be grand and all my problems would be solved. I felt that *Confessions* would be the stepping-stone to more—the beginning of my career and independence. At twenty-six years old I was a best-selling author, debuting at number seven on the *New York Times* best-sellers list and soon rising to number five. I was the toast of my publisher, HarperCollins, while stumping the rest of the publishing world. I felt like the underdog that had finally come from behind to take the cake—the bittersweet cake.

I am often asked by those I call subjournalists, "Are you doing this for the money?" In response I say, "Even the Bible is sold." Why is it that when a little black girl from the islands figures out the key to success, her motives are questioned?

To survive and, finally, to achieve success, I had to go against conventional thinking and do the exact opposite of what others wanted me to do. That meant struggling and finding unorthodox, even unsavory methods to keep my young son and myself above water until I could make my dreams a reality. Organization and the strategic use of opportunity were also key, along with never looking a gift horse in the mouth. Now, after all this perseverance and sacrifice, is my labor not allowed to bear fruit?

Is Bill Gates doing it for the money? Is Donald Trump? The truth is that I enjoy the financial freedom I have made for myself. I am proud finally to have my son's college education paid for, and adequate life, health, and vehicle insurance. Today I own a home and am thrilled at the notion that I will never again have to sleep in my car on a street corner or go without eating. My experiences as a homeless welfare mother are just a few years behind me and still very fresh, reminding me continuously that I have come a long way in a short time. The painful memories of that time have allowed me to accept any and all success with humility. I know I am blessed to have made it out of such harrowing conditions alive, healthy, and with all my faculties intact, and I empathize greatly with other people, especially women, who live their lives, at one point or another, behind the eight ball. However, to whom much is given, much is required. What glitters is very rarely gold and is more often the glimmer of a tin can being kicked down the street by a kid with a dream. Somewhere inside myself, I am still that kid, and there are dreams yet to be realized.

Since becoming something of a public entity I have fought to maintain a sense of modesty and balance. I have dreamed of this since I was five years old, but now I wish I could undo some of what is done. Though I love that my work has been recognized, I am growing increasingly uncomfortable with my *face* being recognized. I recall the days of my youth and the chill I got every time the theme song of *Fame,* the television show, introduced a new episode. I had grandiose visions in my head about what fame would be like: the glamour of fancy clothes, a mansion to live in, private jet rides, and only the most suitable of beaux knocking at my door. I anxiously waited for each episode of *Fame* and screeched along with the voice of Irene Cara belting out its unforgettable theme song, in which she determines to live forever, telling us to remember her name. An old adage comes to mind these days: "Be careful what you ask for—you just might get it."

Life is different for me now in many ways, some that are good and some that just aren't. The places I go and the people I meet along the way evoke a series of notions and introspective, deeply meaningful and life-altering discussions that I never imagined when I was dreaming this dream. I'm offering them to you in much the same form as I tap them into my laptop computer late at night.

Now, with the success of *Confessions,* I find myself delving deeper into Hollywood and rubbing against its underbelly, eyes wide open. I realize now just how naive I was in my first years in this town, smelling only the sweet scent of roses and never noticing the knee-deep horseshit in which they grew. Hollywood is a phantasm, there to delight and delude. It can also be a nasty trap.

The
Vixen Diaries

CHAPTER ONE

A Man Named Norwood

Early in March 2006, Norwood Young invited me to dinner. At first glance, Norwood could be a long-lost brother of Michael Jackson: he must have visited the same plastic surgeon who has sculpted the Jackson kids' imminently recognizable noses and cleft chins. The skin around Norwood's eyes is tight, leading me to believe he's also been nipped and tucked, not just sculpted and dimpled. He also dresses very flamboyantly, with multicolored outfits of exotic materials. His hair is short, black, and wavy, and both ears are adorned with diamond earrings of about six carats. In fact, the earring in his right ear was so heavy, his lobe couldn't bear the weight, and it fell out on several occasions.

Dinner was set for seven at Los Angeles's uber-trendy sushi restaurant Katana, which boasts a full sushi bar, ample, cozy seating in its dimly lit dining room, and a spacious patio overlooking the infamous, fabulous Sunset Strip. A place for the nouveau riche and the celebrity, the eatery shares a building with Miramax Films and boasts a dual staircase leading from the sidewalk onto its outdoor patio and entrance. Inside, Katana is authentically Asian, with a tasteful veneer of Hollywood on top. It's a great place to see famous faces. KISS front man Gene Simmons passed by our table on the way to the men's room as the server brought my second order of hot sake. The sushi bar was packed and became even more alive each time another patron entered the dining room, as the sushi chefs greeted each with a yell. What they were saying is far beyond me, but I could only guess it's Japanese for "Welcome!"

As I said, Norwood is flamboyant; nothing about him is understated. From his fur coat to his designer denim and expensive shoes, it's obvious he has a story to tell. From the second I first saw him, I knew he was different. It takes an unusual man to alter his face to the degree that he has and to dress as outrageously as he does. When Norwood walks into a room, all eyes are on him. Everyone knows he's somebody, but who? He was once the lead singer of an R & B group named Pieces of a Dream, but now no one can pinpoint what he does to support his lavish lifestyle.

Norwood's amazing house is an eyesore to some, and a work of art to others. For those of us who know him, it's a direct reflection of his personality and his own personal, internal revolution. The house, recently featured on the E! series *High Maintenance 90210*, is on one of the busiest corners in Hollywood and is a gaudy display of art and defiance, making it an instant Los Angeles landmark. It is protected by a white decorative gate, and in the driveway is Norwood's late-model Bentley Continental, next to his Lincoln Navigator SUV, painted in an iridescent burnt orange, which changes hues as you walk around it.

But the true attraction of this once average home are the many white replicas of Michelangelo's *David*, historically and infamously naked. The chalk-white forms litter the front yard and even the roof of the home. Though I have not counted them all, there must be at least fifteen statues in the front of the property alone. Not surprisingly, offended neighbors complained and lawsuits were filed, but the statues remain.

I walked up the cobblestone driveway, careful not to ruin the heels of my new stilettos. Norwood met me at the door, but my eyes were not on him as I said hello. They were focused on the painting behind him, an enormous black-and-white self-portrait. The inside of his home is decorated in the same vein as the outside, and to tie it all together, there were two tiny dogs nipping at my heels—one pink, one purple, and aptly named Diva and Divo. There is a strange collection of oversized furniture and artifacts; white lacquer and African masks, neon lights and mirrors all around. Even while standing still, I was spinning, unable to keep my balance. From the curb to the living room, I was already overwhelmed. The closet in his bedroom holds hundreds of outfits on one of those carousel racks that you see at a dry cleaner's!

Norwood and I met on February 22, 2006 on the red carpet for the premier of a little-known film called *Seat Filler*, starring Kelly Rowland, of *Destiny's Child* fame, and Duane Martin, known from the CW series *All of Us*. I guess we didn't actually meet, but we exchanged glances, as if to say, *I see you, you see me, and we're both hot!* Three days later I ran into him again at the GM brunch the morning of the NAACP Image Awards, then later that evening on the red carpet of the Awards. During the brunch we made our first formal introduction with the help of our mutual friends, columnist Jawn Murray and comedian Kim Whitley.

"Karrine, have you met Norwood?" Jawn asked.

"You guys don't know each other?" Kim added.

"No, but I think it's about time we do. I have seen you everywhere!" I replied, offering him my hand.

"Yes, I keep bumping into you. I'm Norwood."

"I'm Karrine. It's a pleasure to meet you finally and officially." By the end of the brunch, he and I had exchanged numbers, which led us to that first night out together at Katana.

It wasn't long before Norwood's story began pouring out of

him, and his truths began to sound strangely familiar. There were many things said at that Katana dinner that I just cannot repeat. As Norwood said, the things he could write a book about would kill his mother, and I don't want to be the one to send Miss Betty over the edge.

What I will say is this: I learned that my story is the story of many women and men alike. Sexual abuse is the hidden secret of many people. Those who were abused as children often grow up with greatly damaged self-esteem coupled with a warped view of sexuality—and many of them get the idea that becoming rich and famous will make all that childhood pain disappear. Perhaps it is not surprising that promiscuity, homosexuality, and just plain sexual confusion runs rampant in Hollywood. Young girls come here hoping to "make it"—and so do young gay men. Who Norwood has slept with and what he has done with them does not amaze me, because we are male and female mirrors, two sides of the same coin. From our lists of liaisons and indecent proposals to the secrets and lies we keep hidden on behalf of those we love, this man and I are twins. However, his stories would not only kill his mother, they would send shock waves through the entire entertainment industry.

Hollywood is a place both of dreams and of scandal. I have lived in this town for over seven years now, and the longer I stay, the more jaded I become—and the more I cannot leave. When I moved here, a friend warned me about the deceptive power of Hollywood. The city seems to be slow paced compared to meccas such as New York, London, Paris, and even Miami, but it is all an illusion. It will lull you to sleep with its palm trees and warm breezes, its beautiful people and casual opulence. And at the exact moment that you relax, the vortex that is Hollywood will suck you in, and your former self will never be seen again.

Hollywood transforms you and makes you into one of *them*. If you're not careful, it's easy to become one of the self-absorbed Beautiful Ones, whose only thrill in life is collecting people and things, as if living in a virtual board game. It becomes impossible for you to fit in anywhere else. Your life revolves around pleasure and beauty— you live your life shopping, exercising, and preserving your youth. Where else is it normal to have your face stretched and your lips puffed up? Where else is having the fat sucked out of your butt and relocated into the crevices of your face a typical lunch-hour appointment? Hollywood is the only place I know where having real breasts is strange and frowned upon, where being an eighty-year-old, wrinkle-free, surgeon-assisted voluptuous former playmate in a new Mercedes Benz SL is a life goal. Hearing the stories of others who live here lets me know that it's not just me; I am not the only one who has changed out of necessity. I am not the only one who has seen and done horrific things in this cesspool of sin.

It is so difficult for people who don't live here to know what Hollywood is like, or to believe the truth about it. And when I say Hollywood, I don't mean the city so much as the lifestyle and frame of mind. When *Confessions of a Video Vixen* was released, I received a lot of initial backlash from people who just couldn't fathom a lifestyle like this: fast money, drugs, and sex—the stuff of which movies are made. But you have to understand that people who know what goes on in this town write the movies we love so much. From *Pretty Woman* all the way to *Boogie Nights*, it's rarely fiction.

As I sat and listened to Norwood, I was reminded of where I was and that this was indeed the land of lost angels. I wondered how much deeper I would sink into this bizarre, materialistic lifestyle. It has already changed me so much. I've gone from bargain-bin shopping to Rodeo Drive, from appreciative to entitled. I have spoiled myself rotten, and I only wonder what I am overcompensating for. Am I still making up for my past and using it as a crutch and an excuse? Or am I just living the good life with "champagne wishes and caviar dreams?"

I felt a connection to Norwood that night as I listened to him tell me about his life, especially the horrible experiences that changed him as a little boy and shaped his manhood. He told me almost unbelievable stories about the double lives of powerful men at the top of the entertainment business in this town, their secrets and lies—things that, if made public, would change their existences and ruin their careers. We spent several hours at Katana that night, letting each other know that we were not alone and, in many ways, not that different. And at the end of it all, it made me think about what my father had said to me long ago about being born a girl. Here before me was a man who had it no better that I had, a man who also lived his life as a vixen and felt the need to do some confessing.

CHAPTER TWO

Rumor Has It

On March 12, 2006, Norwood and I laughed and carried on at a quiet dinner together before heading to actress Lisa Raye's wedding shower. Lisa Raye may be best known for her debut in Ice Cube's film *The Players Club,* and most recently as part of the cast of Jada and Will Smith's recently canceled CW series *All of Us,* but now she was gearing up to marry Michael Missick, the prime minister of Turks and Caicos.

The Asian-themed shower was held at the Eurochow restaurant in Westwood, about four miles from Rodeo Drive. As soon as we made our way through the front door, we were greeted with smiles and hugs. Lisa's half sister, rapper Da Brat, was the first person to say hello and extend an embrace. Then there was Tisha Campbell (*My Wife and Kids*, CW), Tichina Arnold (*Everybody Hates Chris,* CW), Tisha's husband, Duane Martin (*All of Us,* CW), Eddie Murphy's ex-wife, Nicole, with her beau of the moment, and Miss Vivica Fox (*Missing,* Lifetime; and, of course, *Dancing with the Stars,* ABC). Lisa Raye was a vision in a white, Asian silk dress with a casual yet elegant updo. She was warm and sweet as she welcomed me with open arms to her soiree. Vivica was similarly dressed, and greeted me with the same genuine feeling as Lisa, even though she seemed to be jittery and a bit hyper. But that's Vivica, I suppose. She was lovely and pleasant and seemed as if she knew how to party. Even as she danced with her girlfriends, behind her back there were whispers of her recent alleged plastic surgeries.

I overheard one stranger saying, "Thank God she stopped putting that collagen in her lips."

Her friend concurred, "Yeah, but are those cheek and chin implants?"

"I don't know, but that nose job came out all right."

"Yeah, that and the liposuction."

Vivica looked good, and regardless of the surgery rumors, she's a working black actress, which is a lot more than some of the women in that room could say for themselves. And speaking of that, an interesting exchange between Tisha Campbell and Tichina Arnold caught my attention.

After Tichina shared her thoughts with me about my first book, *Confessions of a Video Vixen,* the two of us began a conversation that was both pleasant and enlightening. We were having a great time talking when Tisha interrupted us and demanded to have her friend back.

"Oh!" Tisha said. "Now that you have a show, you're making new friends, and you don't have time to talk to me! I liked you better when you weren't working." Tisha was kidding when she said all this, but even though she was smiling and there was a real sense of levity in her voice, what she said made me think.

I strongly believe that there is truth in everything that is said, and that nothing comes from nowhere. Tisha's statement to Tichina made me wonder: are even your best friends ever really happy for you when you are doing better than they are in the public eye? I wondered if, deep down inside, Tisha really felt this way, even if she didn't realize it. Is Tisha subconsciously jealous of Tichina now that she is on a hit show and Tisha's sitcom was just recently canceled? Maybe, maybe not, but when I see something like that for myself, it makes me wonder about my own friends. Are they really happy for me?

Though I keep in touch with my girlfriends from high school, there is a space between us. There is a difference in lifestyle and life choices. Some of my friends had very few goals and sought only to get married and have children. This plan often goes astray and is a poor substitute for education and personal life goals that do not depend on the well-being and earning ability of another. No woman should have to count on a guy to support her. Some of my friends are successful in their own right but aren't living the lives they once dreamed of, either socially or professionally, and seem to have enormous voids in their existence. I know, everyone's life is different and we all evolve on different levels and at varying times in our lives, so it is not my place or right to judge another's performance in life. But because of our social and economic differences, our conversations are usually one-sided, with me doing most of the talking and having all the eventful accounts, both personal and professional. I often wonder if they are as excited about their lives as they are about my life.

Lisa gave a wonderful speech thanking all her friends and family, and it was at that moment I noticed I had been there too long. Then Jamie Foxx showed up, and I knew it was time to go. Having had the opportunity to spend time with the Oscar winner, I can understand why people, men and women alike, are so drawn to him. He is extremely personable and engaging. His smile is warm and inviting; his jokes are funny, and he rarely acts like the celebrity he is. Jamie has an air of humility, which makes him a people person, that is, one of the people, who doesn't appear to be floating above them. The female guests were swooning and swarming around him.

I could see the few men who were present become uncomfortable as their dates let go of their hands and gravitated toward Jamie.

I could sense a problem on the horizon. Jamie has always been a favorite in black Hollywood, but then, hot on the heels of his Oscar win for his portrayal of Ray Charles in the biopic *Ray*, he was hotter than ever.

After a long night of drinking and dancing, shaking hands and taking pictures, I had had enough, and Norwood shared my sentiment. He and I agreed this would be a good time to sneak out. So as Lisa talked on and Jamie worked his way into the crowd, Norwood and I quietly sneaked out of the venue and headed to the Four Seasons Hotel for a nightcap.

At the Four Seasons, we talked about the evening's events, recapping some of the funnier moments. I thought more about the Tisha and Tichina incident, wondering about the real reason behind it. I thought more about friendship and whether I truly had friends I could trust to be happy for me, even though our lives may take different paths.

It's not as if I hadn't trusted recently, but when I have put my trust in others, that trust has always been broken. There have been disappointments, lies, and unfaithfulness. There have been times in my friendships and romantic relationships when my intelligence was underestimated. My capacity to endure emotional pain has been greatly tested, repeatedly. What I have learned about myself is that often I have been extremely trusting and loving toward those who never deserved it. This in turn has led to my own heartache. I want to learn to trust others again, but first I have to learn to trust myself enough to know who is worthy of such trust, love, and loyalty—and who is not. I am always left confused and brokenhearted when someone in my life proves untrustworthy.

I believe that a part of me is embittered after a lifetime of letdowns and disappointments, and that may be where my strong defiant streak comes from. I certainly have an unwillingness to let new people into my life, and there are times when I am suspicious of the true feelings of the friends I have now. Like most people, I wish to feel safe and at home among the friends in my life. I'd like to know that there are no judgments, jealousies, or ill wishes, and it saddens me to admit that it is a feeling I have yet to possess with certainty.

For example, something interesting was brought to my attention the day after the bridal shower. I was told that despite her light-hearted approach, the real reason Tisha Campbell pulled Tichina Arnold away from me had to do with Larenz Tate. Yes, Larenz Tate, my costar in *A Man Apart*, opposite Vin Diesel and, more recently, part of the cast of the VH1 series *Love Monkey*, as well as the films *Crash* and *Waist Deep*.

On February 22 I had attended the *Seat Filler* premiere and ran into Larenz at the after party. Not having seen him in a few years, I went up to him with my right hand extended and offering a handshake.

"You know I'm mad at you, right?" he griped.

"What?" I reacted in astonishment. "Now, how would I know that when I haven't spoken to you in years?"

"You know, you caused a lot of problems at my house 'cause my name is in that book"—referring to *Confessions*.

I was speechless because his remark was absurd, and frankly, I found it weird. Larenz was mentioned in *Confessions* solely as my costar during the filming of *A Man Apart*. Though I lightly detailed my relationship with Vin, Larenz's mention was nothing but pleasant and very, very brief. There was nothing sexual about it, and frankly, there is nothing scandalous about Larenz to write about—which, in his case, is a good thing. Contrary to what the public may believe, it seems as if only the men who weren't in *Confessions* at all or who were mentioned favorably found fault with the book.

I think it can be quite intimidating for a man to be faced with a woman who is more successful than he is, especially if that woman has been known as a harlot and was counted out years ago. The reality of that must sting, for it most certainly could not have been the passage in *Confessions* where I credited Larenz with helping me in my role as his wife and, along with Vin Diesel and F. Gary Gray, making me feel welcomed on set. All I could do was roll my eyes and walk away laughing.

It seems as if some people want to be important and worthy; therefore, they make something out of nothing in order to flatter themselves. If his wife had an issue with me as he claimed, it was simply her own insecurities. I have never said a bad word about Larenz, nor have I ever found him attractive, especially not while standing next to Vin. A picture of a man and a woman engaged in a friendly embrace in the photo insert of *Confessions of a Video Vixen* does not an affair make—thank God. Nevertheless, it seemed to be the case that Larenz's bogus personal issues took the long way around and made his friend Tisha break up my conversation with Tichina on the night of Lisa Raye's bridal shower.

As I grow as a woman and a public figure, I am finding the strangest characteristics in those around me. Sometimes someone will tell you why they are mad at you, but the reason they give isn't the real source of their anger. And sometimes people will joke about their anger, not realizing or wanting to admit that their jest comes from a real place of discontent inside themselves. I know now that I must keep my eyes open for both types of individuals and, in this distorted town, try to keep my balance.

CHAPTER THREE

On My Own

The *New York Times* best-seller list for the second week of March 2006 positioned *Confessions of a Video Vixen* at number eight, nine months after its debut. The publishing industry called it a phenomenon, yet I still had a hard time grasping the reality of its success—and mine. That Monday, my publicist received two phone calls requesting interviews from me; one from FHM Australia and one from *The O'Reilly Factor* and its host, Bill O'Reilly. This was big, and it was also another time crunch. So there I was on Wednesday, at age twenty-six, preparing for my interview with O'Reilly the next afternoon at three and orchestrating the photo shoot for FHM Australia, which would take place the following Saturday. At this point I had no staff. I was living in a two-bedroom apartment with my son, with a phone and a Blackberry that competed for my attentions all day long.

It was all nerve racking and frantic. O'Reilly is known for his no-holds-barred, no-nonsense approach, and I felt the need to make sure I was up for the challenge. After almost a year of grueling interviews and snappy comebacks, I learned that the best way to combat combativeness was with grace bolstered by information and ammunition, if neccssary. The idea was never to let them see you sweat, never to let them put you on the spot. I rummaged through court documents from a sexual harassment lawsuit filed against him by his former producer, available on TMZ.com, as well as old news clippings about the suit and the settlement that followed. I wanted to be sure I had just as much mud to sling as he did, if he so chose to.

To save money, FHM Australia wanted to use photos from *Vixen* to accompany my two-thousand-word article. I was appalled at the idea. I told them I would shoot my own fresh photos and send them to Australia for print. By taking on that task, I bore the brunt of the expenses, and the sole responsibility for pulling the entire shoot together, all while preparing for O'Reilly.

It was hectic, but I got it done. First I got my glamour squad together. I rang my photographer and clothing, makeup, and hair stylists and made sure everyone would be available on the date I had chosen. Then I picked the location—and paid for it. I chose the Le Meridien in Los Angeles, which had been newly renovated with an Asian flair. Next my stylist and I had to choose a wardrobe. I searched my closet, which I call my clothing library, and pulled several pieces that could be useful for the shoot, ranging from the highly provocative to the plain and demure. My stylist and I went shopping for accessories and wigs to tie all the proposed looks together, while the photographer assembled his equipment, renting what he needed. All this was at my expense, of course, but to me it was important that we achieve the proper look and feel for the photos. All this was happening in an incredibly stressful rush. In a way it was good to be so busy—it helped divert my attention so I could keep my cool about appearing on *The O'Reilly Factor.*

I was scheduled to tape the O'Reilly interview on March 16. At 1:45 in the afternoon, Fox News sent a black Town Car to take me to its studios in Brentwood. As I walked out of my home and onto the driveway I was taken aback by what I saw. The driver of the Town Car was disheveled in appearance, with mussed, wiry hair and dark brown teeth. I'm sure that he introduced himself to me, but I couldn't hear a word he said, because that insistent voice in my head was yelling, "Yuck!" He opened the car door for me, and I slid into the backseat. Yuck again. The inside of the vehicle was filthy, littered with gum wrappers and lint and smelling of cigarettes. This was no luxury sedan. My stomach was filled with butterflies as we made the long, tedious drive to Brentwood. I felt panicky and unsure as I played the upcoming scenario through my head. *What will he say? What will I say? How long will I have to talk to him?*

After hair, makeup, and about fifty peanut butter cheese crackers from the vending machine; it was time for me to find out. Trying to will my stomach to behave, I played it cool as I sat in the solitary chair in the tape room. O'Reilly is located in New York, so I was going to speak to him via satellite. It was hard not to feel a little lonely— there was just one chair, one camera, one microphone, one annoying earpiece, and me. My heart beat fast and heavy in my chest as I settled into position, waiting for O'Reilly to speak into my ear.

"Miss Steffans, can you hear me?" His voice was loud and clear, unmistakably O'Reilly's.

"Yes, I can."

"Good. I'd like to thank you for speaking with me today. Now, I'm not going to go into any of the names in your book—"

"Perfect. Thank you."

"I'll start off asking why you think this book is so important. Is that all right with you?"

"Absolutely. Thank you."

"All right. I want to thank you again for being here, and here we go."

That was all the prep I needed. I was ready to start, get the interview done, and go home. The entire thing was a blur, a whirlwind, and in about six minutes it was all over. I never had to use any of the ammo I'd gathered about the harassment suit. I left the interview shaken, bumming a Pall Mall cigarette from my bedraggled driver. Although O'Reilly was nothing but gracious in the six minutes we had together, I was still a bundle of nerves, wondering how I did and trying to remember what was said.

Most interviews are like that for me. I can never truly remember what I said, and I very rarely watch myself on television. Basically, I just close my eyes and hope for the best. The entire experience is surreal. It's as if I were having an out-of-body experience when I am in an interview or in a red-carpet situation. It's not really me; I am not there. It seems as if the real "me" has met with this "entertainment" me, and when I go home at the end of the night and rest my head, the entire day has been a dream. I wonder if there will be a time in my life and career when I won't be this humble. I mean, there are times when I am a bit bossy, but I am always in awe of my life. I wonder if this will ever seem normal to me.

Just a few days after my O'Reilly experience, the FHM photo shoot went off without a hitch as my team and I worked far into the night. We had been working nonstop, but it paid off. My team made such beautiful music and photos together that FHM Australia reran the pictures and the six-page interview in Spain and Japan. I have also used the photos in several television shows for the E! and VH1 networks, as well as for the German translation of *Confessions*, published in early 2007. I am happy to report that you are also seeing one of the pictures from that session on the cover of this book!

Score one big win for preparation! All the money I'd spent getting ready for the shoot was more than worth it. The long, arduous hours paid off. They took me a step higher in my career and just that much closer to where I want to be, not just as an author but as an entrepreneur, a woman who can run her life and her business with ease, grace, and expertise. This is both the curse and the blessing of being an entrepreneur; I sometimes feel like a one-woman show, but that's the way it has to be if I am to take responsibility for making my life and career what I want them to be: successful and enduring. I do not work alone, but I am sure to do most of the work myself— the curse of an imperfect perfectionist.

CHAPTER FOUR

On Tour

As part of my media tour, I appeared on the *Tyra Banks Show*. It was not a good experience—I found Tyra to be both a hypocrite and a member of a thriving but overlooked breed of female chauvinists. While waiting backstage to be introduced on her CW talk show, I was appalled to hear her giving a little speech to her audience and viewers. In effect, she was setting me up. She rattled off a disclaimer, stating that she in no way agreed with or supported *Confessions*—or me. Leave it to a model to take the low road where actual journalists have not. And this is not just any model, but a model who has dated in the same circles that I have. She attacked me for "exploiting" the men in my book and for dating celebrities, and yet, Tyra gushed over Dennis Rodman, another guest on the show, celebrating his exploits and asking questions about Madonna and Carmen Electra. Why wasn't he bashed for dating celebrity women and displaying his private life?

After the break I questioned Tyra about her approach. "I am a celebrity first, and these are my colleagues," she told me. Colleagues—in the fashion industry? Funny, I've never seen Bobby Brown or Vin Diesel on a runway in a thong. Or was this just model-speak for

"We've slept with some of the same guys"? And shouldn't she want to be a woman first? Whatever happened to women's solidarity? Tyra missed the boat and the opportunity to draw from the message in *Confessions*, but in the words of Maya Angelou, "still I rise." You can bank on that.

My session with Donny Deutsch, host of *The Big Idea* on CNBC, was more of the same. Deutsch continuously badgered me about the celebrity men I mentioned in *Confessions*, Shaquille O'Neal in particular. If the celebrities included in the book did not speak up for themselves, why was Deutsch so upset on their behalf?

On this particular program, the stench of chauvinism was in the air, and the hypocrisy flag was flying high. Hugh Hefner was a guest on the same show, and Deutsch lavishly praised his "idol." In Donny's words, I was "exploiting" the men in my book, but Hugh was "the man." I've made a living, in part, by exposing and displaying men I have slept with. Hugh has made a fortune, in part, by exposing and displaying women, many of whom he has slept with, yet I am to be ashamed and Hefner is to be praised. Hey, Deutsch, what's the big idea? Hey, Deutsch, what's the big difference? Here was the double-stupid double standard at its worst, something I became all too familiar with during my *Confessions* publicity tour.

These two experiences were in marked contrast with my experience with Oprah Winfrey. On April 4 I found myself in Chicago, at the entrance to Harpo Studios, home of the legendary Oprah Winfrey and her precedent-setting talk show. Compared to any other television show, Oprah treats her guests first class, but none of it seemed to faze me as we got out of the clean, comfortable limousine and passed through Harpo's glass entrance. With me on this trip were Gilda, my HarperCollins publicist; Norwood, who took care of my hair, makeup, and wardrobe; and my good friend from Alabama, Deneen.

It was just two weeks earlier that I received a phone call from

Gilda while in the bakery aisle of my local supermarket. Immediately on hearing her voice, I knew she had good news—better news than she'd ever had. It was all on the verge of bursting out of her when she asked me if I was sitting down.

"No," I replied, "And if I did, I'd probably be carted off to the crazy house. Right now I'm wheeling a shopping cart through the grocery store, but I'll pull over. What's up?"

"I just got a call from the producers at Oprah."

"And . . . ?"

"And they want you on the show!"

I'm not sure if what I felt could be categorized as excitement, since it felt a lot more like relief. Certainly, standing in a busy grocery store didn't make it any easier for me to express myself on hearing the news. I stood there by the English muffins in aisle 7, stuck. My eyes grew misty, and a tear made its way from the inside corner of my left eye as I came face-to-face with a goal and dream realized. After a pregnant pause, Gilda checked my vitals. "Are you there?"

"Okay. Here we go."

"Yep. Here we go!"

I was instructed to keep the upcoming taping a secret and not to tell even my closest friends. This was fairly easy to do, except that I had to tell one person: my ex-boyfriend, mentor, and confidant Bill Maher. I gave myself time to live with the news alone, then left the message on his answering machine a couple of days later. For the next week and a half, I prepared for my appearance on *Oprah*, just as I had since I was a little girl back when this dream began—only this time it was for real.

I expected to be nervous and overjoyed at the idea of sitting down with the most influential woman in media, but as we walked into the studio, surprisingly, I was calm and introverted. Norwood had his game face on—he was serious about his business of making sure my physical appearance was flawless. Gilda was a nervous wreck. She slipped me a handful of notes written on tiny little pieces of paper to remind what to say and what not to say. I politely tucked the notes into my purse, knowing that no one could help me now. I was going to sit next to Oprah Winfrey, and all the coaching in the world would not prepare me for the drastic turn my life was about to take.

Once in the green room, Norwood laid out his supplies and got to work on my face. Over the next hour, I sat in a chair while everyone fussed over me. Gilda was wringing her hands, Deneen was praying over me, and Norwood kept turning my head this way and that. It was all a bit too much, and I began to feel overwhelmed.

It got worse when a pair of Oprah's producers began taking turns briefing me on what I was supposed to say once I got onstage. These two pleasant young women did their jobs impeccably and almost to a fault, but whatever they were saying went in one ear and out the other, completely bypassing my brain. In the back of my mind I was thinking, *Would you just get out of my face and stop trying to tell me what to say and think?* As much as they tried to convince me that portions of the show are loosely scripted, I knew that nothing in my life ever goes as expected—and, in fact, usually goes a lot better than anyone could ever have hoped. My only hope was that this experience would be no different.

Everything was moving around me at lightning speed, and it was all I could do not to cry. Finally, I exploded. "I hate my hair! Don't talk to me! Stop touching me! Everyone shut up!" It all detonated just moments before I was to join Oprah onstage. My hair was huge and reminiscent of a piece from the Dolly Parton wig collection, which made me wonder if Norwood had a drag queen living inside him that's just dying to get out. Deneen was rebuking the devil and touching me all over as if performing an exorcism, and Gilda just kept handing me tiny pieces of paper with chicken-scratched notes on them.

Just as I was melting down, I was pulled from the green room and onto the stage. I was a mess up until the very moment I saw her enter the studio. Making her way to the stage, she waved easily to the audience as they jumped to their feet in exhilaration, screaming and carrying on, some with tears in their eyes. As I sat there watching this, I could feel the love, all of it directed toward Oprah, and as I continued to watch in awe I whispered to myself, "I want this."

It is by pure example that Oprah inspires me. Even if I don't agree with everything she says and does, it doesn't change the fact that she is a woman affecting lives and changing the world for the better, wherever and however she can. She is one who came from nothing and endured some of the same abuses I have; she's also made a few of the same mistakes. She never let her past get in the way of her future. She worked diligently to become influential, and remains purpose driven both despite and because of her success. As I watched her walk onto that soundstage, I knew then how far I wanted to go and that there is really no limit to the things I could accomplish. I also realized that there is no reason to be afraid of what is to come.

Because I am a naturally anxious person, I have always feared success, thinking it meant only that I was coming closer to my death. I have always felt that if I go too far, too fast, it means that the end is not only inevitable but just around the corner. And just as soon as this thought enters my mind, I remind myself of the devil's work. I remind myself that if I am meant for greatness, there will be efforts made to stop me, and death is surely one way to do it. Waiting for Oprah as she welcomed everyone to the show, all that went out the window. I wasn't afraid of dying; I wasn't afraid of the prospect of my success. Instead I inhaled the idea of it, the feeling of accomplishment and purpose, and the power of love.

I rose to my feet as Oprah turned to me, arms outstretched. As she welcomed me with her embrace, I welcomed all my answered prayers. I had been dreaming of this moment since I was a young girl. I would lock myself in the bathroom at home and practice my Oprah cry—the way my face would look when she evoked emotion in me, which, I knew, she would. I practiced what I would talk about and how I would sit. I always pictured myself in a silk top and a pencil skirt, the type women wore in the old black-and-white films I loved so much as a girl. I had pictured it all in my head twenty years ago, and here it was, the moment I had waited for all my life.

Just as I had pictured it, I wore a deep fuchsia silk blouse and a white pencil skirt along with a fabulous pair of shoes, which were too tight to actually walk in but were perfect for sitting with the queen of daytime, a shoe lover.

"Cute shoes!" Oprah said as she sat next to me on the sofa.

Inside, I gave a little cheer—my strategy had worked. I had planned my footwear carefully, hoping to grab her attention. "Oh, thank you," I said in a voice that I hoped sounded casual and unassuming. "My toes are numb, but I look fabulous!" We laughed in unison for a brief moment; then it was on to business.

For the next twenty-two minutes, she and I had a delightful exchange. For the first time since publishing *Confessions,* I felt I was with someone who understood, someone who was not condemning me, someone who recognized pain and the effects of trauma. For the first time I was not alone in my thoughts and truths. My experience with Oprah was the complete opposite of my experience with Donnie Deutsch and Tyra Banks. She was not judgmental but understanding—when I cried, she cried, and when she touched me, I touched her and felt at home in her light.

I left Chicago with a sense of accomplishment and an overall feeling of calm. I had done what I came to do. I told my story, denouncing my demons, and took it all to the queen. I was done and ready for a break. On the flight home I thought of traveling abroad, touring Europe: London, Paris, Italy. More than anything, I am beginning to long for a new place in the world. Fame is nothing I thought it would be. Very little of it is glamorous, and for every person who loves you, there are two who don't. The good thing about this life is that I can feel my skin thickening and my heart growing more empathetic. In its own way, this new life of mine, grueling though it may be at times, is helping to turn me into the woman I have always wanted to be: a woman comfortable in her own skin and growing increasingly unaffected by other people's expectations and thoughts of her.

I have most certainly learned the difference between journalists who conduct an interview to get responses from me that inform and benefit the viewing and listening audience, and subjournalists who blurt out questions to call attention to themselves and drum up ratings through confrontation. Appearing with Oprah presented more than just the realization of a dream for me. It broadened my horizon and set the bar even higher for what I should expect—what I have a right to expect—in my dealings with the press.

Chapter Five

Teddy Pendergrass?

y appearance on *Oprah* aired on Monday, April 10, 2006, the day before I was to travel to Arkansas for a speaking engagement at Philander Smith College. It was 2:55 in the afternoon, and I was running late to Norwood's, where I had reluctantly agreed to watch myself on the show—something I very rarely do. About fifteen minutes into my drive, my cell phone rang. I gave it a curious look when I realized that the call was from Harpo Studios.

"Hello, is this Karrine?"

"It is . . ."

"Hi, this is Kim at Harpo Studios. Your episode has already aired on the East Coast. Shortly after it ended, we received a call from Teddy Pendergrass. He watched the show, thought you were amazing, and would like me to give you his number if you'd like to call him."

"What? Oh, okay. Give it to me."

My first conversation with Teddy took place several hours after I received the call from Harpo, and lasted a little over an hour. At first Teddy was full of praise, offering congratulations for the way

I spoke and represented my life, past and present. It is not completely unusual for a celebrity to reach out to me and offer his or her opinion or praise. When those kinds of calls come, they usually last just a few minutes—and however sincere we are when we vow to keep in touch, we rarely do. We hold that thought and keep up the intention of staying in touch, though. Therefore, when we see each other out and around town, we act as if we were long-lost friends, too busy to make the call, though it is on our minds every day. This is the Hollywood way, and this is the way I expected my introduction to Teddy would go.

That first phone call, though a bit long, was uneventful. I listened intently to Teddy as he told me a few bits and pieces about his life, hoping to learn something from this fifty-six-year-old man who, as he revealed to me, was recovering from cancer of the tonsils. As he spoke, I imagined him in his wheelchair, being attended to by the people I heard swarming around him. I wondered what his life was like. I especially wondered whether he had a sex life—more so after he told me that he didn't pick up the phone thinking, "Yeah, I'm gonna knock them boots."

I tilted my head much like my curious Yorkshire terrier, not for just one reason but for two. It had been about thirteen years since I'd heard the term "knocking boots," and I could only imagine that this man, pretty much twice my age, was using it as an attempt to connect with my youth. Unfortunately for Teddy, he was connecting more with my gag reflex, especially at the mere thought of the two of us having sex—which brings me to the second reason why I was confused. Because he is a quadriplegic, Teddy has no control or function of his muscles from the chest down. I wondered if being paralyzed that way affected his arms, or just his torso and lower half. In other words, I wondered if it included the muscle with which he would "knock boots," but I was afraid to ask.

A few days later, I was surprised to hear from Mr. Pendergrass yet again. This phone call, however, lasted for over two hours, and the content of it was a lot more than I bargained for. As I stayed on the line reluctantly, Teddy rambled on.

"This is divine intervention—God's plan," he told me fervently. "I mean, how else can you explain it? I want to make you happy, and I know you can make me happy. Come to Philadelphia. I would like you to be my guest at the Rhythm and Blues Awards, and at another award ceremony where the Urban League is honoring me. As a matter of fact, why don't you come to Philly next week? And you can bring your son if you have to."

This caught me off guard. I put him off, saying, "Ummm . . . I don't know. I'd have to check my schedule," but honestly, I was appalled. His offer came from out of the blue, after an entirely innocent first conversation. After meeting me over the phone just days before, he was inviting me on trips and asking me to be his date at very public appearances in his hometown. I was immediately turned off by his approach, and while he continued I made up my mind never to speak to him again.

Teddy has called several times since then, but I've kept my promise to myself not to take his calls. It seemed as if he had gotten the impression that because of my past I am at a loss for male companionship, attention, and love—either that or I'm just bored, with too much time on my hands. It doesn't matter one way or another: whether he thinks I'm needy, or he is needy himself. In either case, I'd prefer to leave our brief acquaintance where it is: in the past.

When Teddy Pendergrass first reached out to me I thought, *How harmful can this be? He's incapacitated, so sex just can't be an issue. It's been a very long time since he was hot on the charts, so he couldn't be looking for a comeback*—or could he? I thought Teddy would be a harmless long-distance acquaintance, of which I have many. But when he asked me to be his guest at two separate functions just a week apart, I began to second-guess his motives. Sounded to me as if he had "knocking boots" on his mind all along.

Now, there may have been a time in my past when I would at

least have considered his offer as a way to put bread on my table and provide for my son, but that was my old life, the life before *Confessions*—the life I have chosen to leave behind. Having my own financial security means having the power to say yes or no in any interaction with the opposite sex, free of any financial considerations. That choice is mine alone to make, and because I know what it has cost me to get to a level where I can make that choice, I'm not giving it up.

After *Confessions of a Video Vixen* was published, the word "groupie" was thrown at me a lot, as I am sure it still is in certain circles. I've never been quite sure what the word means these days, but it was originally applied to young women who followed and lusted after music groups—and the bands usually lusted right back, especially when they were on the road.

In the 1980s, however, the Bangles made it painfully obvious that men can be and often are groupies as well, as documented in a now infamous sex tape featuring several of their most devoted groupies. These days, the word itself has come to imply automatically that the groupie in question is a woman, and in urban circles it seems to be slapped on any woman who is acquainted with celebrities.

Very rarely is it discussed that men can also be groupies, but now I seem to have attracted a following of my own—not that it's a following I want. You know how, when someone wins the lottery, all their long-lost relatives come out of the woodwork? That's how it has been for me.

Over the past year I have witnessed many of the men from my past resurface and try to latch on to my fame and success. All of a sudden, the ex-boyfriend who told me I would be nothing without him says he cannot live without me. The guy who told me that he and his family were better than I was because I was flat broke and they had millions now rings my phone several times a week, asking for a date and a second chance. Those who once said I was nothing to them somehow found it in their hearts to fall in love with me, claiming they always were.

I think many people are under the impression that because of my scandalous reputation I have been blacklisted in both my professional and personal life. Those who think so have no idea how wrong they are. I have never been more sought after than I am right now, and though some young women would be flattered by the attention, I have to admit, it makes me ill. I can only imagine that the reason for this resurfacing is nothing more than the power of suggestion and publicity. Society today is such that when someone is on television and becomes newsworthy, they instantly become more attractive and desirable.

Disturbingly obvious evidence of this is the most recent Flava Flav invasion. Here is a man who has a bushel of children by several different women; who had a difficult time providing for his children before his recent success, and who, by the way, may just be one of the most unattractive men in the world. Inexplicably, women are falling over themselves to meet this man. It can't be his good looks, and though it may be his charm, his gold teeth and the wall clock around his neck cancel all that out—or they should. It's the show and all that new money—that's what people are attracted to. Why should I believe I am any different, that my exes all of a sudden came to their senses and see me as I am? I'd be a fool to believe.

Chapter Six

College Drop-In

One day after the airing of my *Oprah* episode, I was in Arkansas of all places, with Deneen in tow. Even though I often joke that it took me two planes and a donkey to get to Philander Smith College in Little Rock, it was a trip that warmed my heart and taught me a great deal about my purpose in life.

Founded in 1877, Philander Smith is one of the oldest private black colleges in the United States. Its mission is to educate young men and women who have the potential to be academically talented, regardless of their income and upbringing, and to help them reach their potential as human beings. This was my first time speaking, and here I was at a university—I, who never even graduated from high school—and the fact that someone wanted me to speak to kids who are smart enough to go to university made me feel hypocritical.

Arriving at the college, I was surprised to learn how small it was—the entire student body consists of just 850 students. I was greeted with open arms by Dr. Walter Kimbrough, president of the college, a man who is often referred to as the "hip-hop president" because he makes use of pop culture references in his teaching and lectures. With him were several students, and together we went off to a buffet dinner. At first the students and I were sort of in awe of one another. I kept thinking that they were doing something that I've never done—getting a higher education—and they were looking at me and thinking that I was doing things they'd never done.

After the meal and small talk were over, I addressed a full house in the lecture hall. Standing on the stage, staring out into the crowd and blinded by the spotlight, I was momentarily at a loss for words. I had not practiced beforehand, because I did not want to sound rehearsed. I generally prefer to speak from my heart and in the moment, but in this instance I started having second thoughts about the wisdom of that choice. I searched for the words to say what I thought was important to these kids, and silently prayed I would not fumble. Once again, my conscious state took a backseat to my subconscious, and the words just rolled from my mouth. There is never a theme to my lectures, unless specified by my host, so I often find myself bouncing off questions from the crowd and speaking to issues that concern them. At Philander the subjects skipped around, from dating to the manipulation of music and the media, and from the diamond crisis in West Africa to the feticides in India and Darfur.

Wherever the group led, I followed, wanting to touch on topics of importance to them. After an hour-long talk, I was met with cheers and applause throughout the auditorium, followed by a long line of students waiting for me outside the hall to sign their copies of *Confessions*. I can't remember everything I said to the students of Philander Smith College, but whatever it was, it must have been appreciated. My parting was just as warm as my reception, but just as I thought it was time to head back to my hotel, I found I was meant to serve an even greater purpose.

It's one thing to speak in generalities to a large group of students, but quite another to sit face-to-face with a few young people and be given the responsibility of offering them advice and answers to their most pressing personal questions. Dr. Kimbrough and I convened after the lecture, along with many of the original group of students I had met over dinner a couple of hours earlier. Several girls pulled me aside and told me secrets about themselves. One girl showed me how she'd burned herself. Self-mutilation like this is rooted in a severe lack of self-esteem, and most of those who attempt it are young women. They try—unsuccessfully—to substitute physical pain for emotional anguish. Often this torment manifests itself by cutting or burning one's skin. Others turn to promiscuity or drug abuse. It's merely a way to divert the pain, temporarily making it go away.

That was the day I realized that I have a responsibility. When *Confessions* came out, people began throwing stones at me, calling me all kinds of "harlot," branding a scarlet "A" on my chest—or forehead. In the midst of all that public accusation, I found my purpose—in the middle of spit bucket Arkansas with kids who were just trying to get an education and a chance at a better life. I suddenly understood why I was there.

As I spoke to these young women, tears came to their eyes. I not only felt the pain they were in but also identified with it on a personal level. I know firsthand what it's like to hurt that much inside— what's it's like to want that pain to leave your body so desperately that you create ways for it to do so. There are still days when I think, *Why am I doing this? Why am I setting myself up for all this?* That was the day that gave me the answer.

It is so difficult for young women to articulate what is wrong— why they are unhappy or unfulfilled. Many of us know we don't feel well at times, but don't have the proper language to put a name to it. Often we are not aware that what we are experiencing is really quite common and nothing to be ashamed of—that with a bit of help we can begin to understand our feelings and know what to do when they arise again.

I was happy and honored, as I always am when young women trust me with their darkest secrets and ask me for a bit of encouragement and guidance. I told these young women what I tell so many others: "Talk about it. Tell someone how you feel, and be honest with yourself about where the hurt comes from. If nothing else, you have each other." For the next thirty-five minutes we stood apart from the rest of the group as they offered their truths and I comforted them with the best advice I could give.

When we were finished, I sat to sign books and flyers for the students and president. A young man sat next to me and asked me if I minded giving him advice as well. I was flabbergasted and overwhelmed with pride and humility all at once. As I looked this young man in the eyes, I pictured my own son at nineteen years old—just ten short years from now—needing advice about girlfriends and peer pressure. I was a bit misty as I gave him advice. I told him that regardless of whether your friends like your girlfriend, if the woman you are with screams, points, and spits, then she is not a lady and is most likely not the type of woman you want to be with, nor does she deserve you. I could see the lightbulb go on inside his head, and that he knew just what I meant.

There was also another young man who wanted to know what advice I could give him about being steadfast in his goals and dreams. This was something I had thought a lot about. "Every day when you wake up," I told him, "only do the things that you know will bring you closer to your dreams. Write a list and follow it: books to read, people to meet, places to go. Whatever it takes, do it and do nothing else, because every time you wake up and waste the day, you're wasting your life, so you may as well be dead. And which of us wants to be dead?"

"That's good shit. Thank you. Really, thanks." He wore dark

blue baggy jeans and a red T-shirt. His hair was in cornrows, and his teeth plated in yellow gold—not stereotypically collegiate in the slightest. But there he was, wanting more out of life, wanting success, and hungering for any advice he could get on how to achieve it. I gave him a hug and wished him well before sliding into my waiting Town Car. I will never forget the people I met at Philander Smith College and what they have taught me. In the humblest surroundings you'll find the most magnificent blessings, and the people you'd never think could inspire you often do exactly that.

It was a hassle getting to Little Rock; I was under enormous pressure to perform, and though I feel I could have done a whole lot better, the university's faculty seemed impressed with what I had to say. I never want to get too full of myself; I love the feeling of being surprised when people are impressed by me. It keeps me focused, modest, and diligent. In the back of my mind, I had been wondering if it was all worth it, but speaking with these students convinced me that it was.

CHAPTER SEVEN

My Space

O ver the past few years, friends have been telling me about the Web site MySpace and how much fun it is, but when I turned on the news, all I ever heard was about the danger—how sexual predators, deviants, and maniacs were cyber-masquerading there as teens to lure young boys and girls into real-life sexual encounters. This did not make me want to hop online and race to MySpace, but then I saw a story about Joe Rogan, host of *Fear Factor,* and his brutal verbal exchange with a member of the site. This little news piece was in every celebrity news report, and I have to admit that it was the sole occurrence that prompted me to visit MySpace to see what all the hoopla was about.

Initially I was curious about why Joe Rogan would take all this time and energy to go back and forth with a fan in these long-drawn-out childish exchanges. Like many other visitors, I went through the blogs and found them reminiscent of my junior high years. My curiosity quickly waned, but I figured that since I was already on MySpace, I might as well stay awhile and look around. Within minutes, I found some of my closest friends and a few people I didn't know but wanted to—friends of friends, whom I found attractive and interesting.

I met electronically with friends like columnist Jawn Murray, the infamous villainess Omarosa (the woman you loved to hate from *The Apprentice*), and cartoonist Aaron McGruder (*The Boondocks*). Then I came across a couple of people I didn't know yet but, for one reason or another, wanted to.

One was love song crooner Eric Benét, (now more famous for his failed marriage to Academy Award winner Halle Berry). For the first week or so after we met online, Eric and I exchanged e-mails, text messages, photographs, friendly gestures, and innuendos. It was all very innocent and not intended to lead anywhere, except to a friendship based on a couple of mutual friends. Those friends kept encouraging us to meet in person. Because he was working in Puerto Rico when our correspondence began, we made plans to get together for lunch when he returned.

We met at Hugo's Restaurant in Sherman Oaks; just moments from his home and mine. I parked in the lot and waited in my car until I saw his BMW pull into a space a few feet away. Eric was warm and inviting as we shared a tentative embrace in the parking lot. After a little over a week of talking by text, this was the first time I'd actually heard his voice.

I ordered a salad; he had soup. The fare and the conversation were light, though the tension was high. First meetings are always awkward, but doing so under the watchful eye of fifty perfect strangers is even more uncomfortable. We were seated at a table in the middle of the restaurant, and it felt as if all eyes were on us, because they were. With my first book and his high-profile broken marriage, it seemed as if we were surrounded by fifty pairs of eyes ready to see the worst in both of us. I could just imagine the gossipy whispers: *"So she was the one who broke up that marriage,"* or *"I bet he's in her book somewhere."* Nevertheless, we ignored what we thought people might be saying about us and began to talk quietly about ourselves—me and my book tour, him and his efforts to build a new life for himself after

Halle. And everyone wonders what kind of idiot would step out on Halle Berry. I look at it differently. In order for a man to be unfaithful to Halle Berry, does he *have* to have something wrong with him?

People make mistakes that hurt other people, and it broke my heart to hear him tell how badly it ended. You don't have to be a sex addict to cheat on your wife: you just have to be a really bad husband. The betrayal of a spouse or loved one is often devastating, no matter how beautiful, famous, or wealthy you may or may not be. Just because someone is beautiful, famous, and wealthy doesn't make her exempt from this betrayal, nor does it make her betrayer sick. It just means that she deserves better, and that he deserves whatever he's left with after she's gone.

The things he shared with me will remain private. I don't ever want to feel that I have violated the trust he showed. Contrary to popular belief, I have never told all, not in *Confessions,* not in this book, and not in my actual life. As for Eric and me, that lunch was the beginning of a mild but uneventful friendship, the sort of friendship that warms you at crowded Hollywood functions when you peer across the room and are relieved to see a familiar face looking back, smiling. After countless phone calls, e-mails, nights out, and visits to my home, we remain friendly yet distant.

Thanks to MySpace, I also had the pleasure of getting to know Andy Dick—electronically, that is. Although it may be surprising to many people, I never found Eric sexy, but I find Andy Dick extremely sexy—go figure. I certainly had heard interesting "facts" about him. At this time, I can only count it as gossip, but the word around town is that Mr. Dick has a big one, at least according to one of his alleged male lovers. Wow. Owen Wilson would be jealous—trust me.

Over the past two years Andy and I have exchanged a series of e-mails sharing each other's latest news, trials, and tribulations. I talk about work and boredom, and he brings me up to speed on his business affairs and his battle to stay alcohol free. We tell silly jokes and amuse each other through our e-mails. It's become a strange phenomenon, this relationship Andy and I have, because neither of us wants to meet in person. There is something fanciful and intriguing about having a pen pal who lives in your city, someone you could bump into at any time at any party in Hollywood.

By his own admission, Andy is bisexual and lives with both his boyfriend and girlfriend. With Andy, I wasn't surprised when he told me about his sexual proclivities. In fact, I was actually quite impressed that he was honest enough to tell me about it. A lot of men are running around living double lives and not telling anyone. That's wrong—if that's the way you're living your life, you need to have that conversation with your partner or partners, and with your friends as well. These are issues that should be introduced early in a friendship, since you never know where things may go.

Andy told me this in casual conversation, but we live in a town where people don't always do that. Men these days will tell you everything else about themselves *except* that they're gay, or bi, or having sex with multiple partners. It happens so much in the music industry, in the rap world, in entertainment in general. I've had five or six boyfriends like that in the past—you walk in on your boyfriend, and there he is, in bed with his basketball buddy. One ex-boyfriend of mine, who was the lead singer of an R & B threesome, kept a bunch of soaps and razors made for women in his bathroom. For months I thought he lived with a woman and just didn't want to tell me. I eventually found out that the products were his and that his business manager was his lover. Another ex, a music television personality, also has a business manager who doubles as his lover. Just recently, a good girlfriend of mine discovered that her ex, a member of the Minnesota Vikings, was on the down low.

That's a lot worse than just cheating on someone. If you're a woman and someone you're seeing is switch-hitting and not telling you, it's a very, very dangerous thing. The phenomenon of barebacking is something that I want women to know about. For those who are unaware, barebacking means unprotected gay anal sex. If both men are monogamous and neither is infected with HIV, it's not a problem, but that's not what it's usually about. Barebacking has become associated with risky sexual behavior, now more than ever. There are increasing numbers of gay men who actually want to contract the disease, and actively seek out HIV positive partners so that they too can become HIV positive. They're known as "bug chasers," and they call the disease "the gift." You may think it's more than a little twisted, but it's considered by some gays to be a badge of belonging, like joining a gang and wearing the colors. Barebacking parties, or "conversion" parties, are functions in which HIV- and AIDS-infected homosexual males meet with other men who are not yet infected. At these underground gatherings, no condoms are allowed, and infected men have sex with those who are not in hopes of giving them the gift.

In places like Hollywood, where the line between gay and straight is more than a little blurry, this has become a huge issue for women. Many of these men are on the down low—in their public life they date women or are married. As a result, women's chances of contracting the deadly disease are increasing, and they have no clue that they're in danger.

There are so many women who want to be here so badly, so many women who want to live this lifestyle, and they have no idea what they're getting into. To me it's another signal to be very careful about who I'm dating, since people are strange and do strange things. It's always better to know who and what your partner is.

The last person I met on MySpace was someone I never expected to find, someone who helped close a gap in my life. During the last few weeks of December 2006, I began to feel very nostalgic, as many of us do during the holiday season. I combed MySpace, wondering what ever happened to my best friend from middle school.

Her name was Deana, and we met when we were just eleven years old and in the sixth grade at Lomax Middle School in the Tampa Bay area. She was new to town, hailing from Indiana, and I was an arrogant, unhappy child who had made a name for herself by being mean to every little girl she met. I had not been there much longer than Deana—I had recently moved from St. Thomas with my mother and two younger sisters. Because I always felt out of place and very different from the children I met in Florida, I covered my discomfort at being an outsider by being brash and sassy.

Deana was no more comfortable in her new home than I was, and there was something about her that put me at ease. We became the best of friends, but our friendship was cut short when Deana and her mother moved to Zephyrhills, another town in Florida. Still the outsider, I was alone and friendless once more. I remember crying for her and feeling even more out of place than I had before I met her. She was the only girl my mother would allow me to spend time with away from home; we enjoyed weekend trips to the beach and the lake, staying over in hotels and lake houses. I'd never had so much fun or enjoyed many firsts as with Deana. I never forgot her or what our friendship meant to me.

Seventeen years later, in the middle of a sleepless night, I searched for her on MySpace. I thought it was a crazy idea and probably a long shot, but it was worth a try. I wondered if she'd married and had children by now. I wondered whether I would recognize her as a grown-up. I remembered that she had beautiful dark hair and a perfectly symmetrical face with perfectly shaped eyebrows. Growing up, I always thought she was so much prettier than I. I searched her maiden name and came up with nothing. Then I searched her first name only, within one hundred miles of Tampa. My search turned up pages upon pages of Deanas in the Tampa Bay area, but none of them fit the description, until I came to one of the last, and there she was—or at least I thought so.

Dark hair, symmetrical face, and beautifully shaped eyebrows, living in Tampa, age twenty-eight—this had to be her! When I clicked on her picture, however, I discovered that her MySpace page was private. As a result I couldn't retrieve any personal information such as where she went to high school, or more pictures of her and her family. There was nothing I could pull up on the computer that would help me determine whether this was my friend. Not knowing for sure, I decided to send this Deana an e-mail and ask if, by any chance, she could be the little girl I knew in middle school. In my heart, I was afraid this wasn't her. I was convinced I was wrong and that this perfect stranger would tell everyone what a nut Karrine Steffans is! I turned off my laptop, folded it shut, and slid it under my bed, putting Deana and my days in Tampa out of my mind for the night.

The next morning was like any other as I awoke with the sun and proceeded to open all the windows, let the dogs out, and light the scented candles placed throughout the house. I turned on the morning news for a bit and then opened my laptop to check messages and send my usual morning e-mails to my attorney, my accountant, and the like. After that, I checked my MySpace page, and saw a reply to the e-mail to Deana that I had sent the night before. I opened it with trepidation—I was afraid that it wasn't her, and at the same time I was afraid that it was. If this really was Deana, my past and present would be joined, and this part of my life would come full circle. What was old would be new again, and as thrilling as the thought was, I was very nervous to know if this was *my* Deana.

And so she was, and suddenly I was eleven years old all over again. Within minutes, we were on the phone together, laughing, crying, and reminiscing about the girls we used to be. In a way, it was as if no time had passed—Deana and Karrine were BFF once again! We made plans to see each other in the near future. Then we caught up on what had happened to each of us since we last spoke seventeen years earlier. Deana was now a newlywed with two children. She shared stories about her new life, and we swapped funny memories about our past.

Oddly enough, even though she had seen my book, she had never put two and two together. It was not until I sent her the e-mail that she was able to make the connection. I was nervous about what she thought about *Confessions* and about me. She told me that before she knew that *that* Karrine Steffans, the author of *Confessions,* was her best friend, she passed judgment on me as almost everyone did, thinking I had made it all up. She also explained that knowing what my home life was like back then, she wasn't surprised that I got onto the wrong path in my late teens and early twenties. She went on to tell me that now, knowing that this was the same girl from her childhood, she could no longer judge me unfairly. Deana was there during some of the most heartbreaking moments of my young life, which means that as an adult she understood, and that is something only a friend can do. At a time in my life when I do believe that it is better to understand than to be understood, I also believe that a bit of the latter is nice, too.

So many things and people in my life have come and gone, and there is hardly anyone from my girlhood whom I can talk to. Luckily I have found a group of beautiful friends in recent years who support and love me, but there is something to be said for the love of a friend who knew you before you knew yourself, when you could count the years of your life on your fingers and you were too short to reach your mother's liquor stash without a chair.

So here's to Deana and to MySpace—a place for friends. I tapped into MySpace in search of other people and wound up finding a piece of myself.

CHAPTER EIGHT

How to Save a Life, Part One

As April 2006 wrapped up, I was looking forward to two months of writing and introspective quiet time. The month had started off with a huge high, my appearance on *Oprah*, but toward the end of it I felt as if I had crashed and burned. I started second-guessing myself. I wondered if I was doing the right things. In my late twenties, I feel too young to know what's really good for me, and too old to make critical mistakes. This is the life I have asked for since I was young, but now that it is mine, I am uncomfortable in it at times.

I am so afraid of going backward that I am ever vigilant and hypersensitive to all that goes on around me. I want to be sure to make the right decisions as I go forward, but knowing that I am human scares me. It means that I am vulnerable and prone to mistakes and even personal disaster. A friend of Bobby Brown's stopped me outside my son's school. It's always uncomfortable for me when running into people from my past, no matter how friendly they may be, and seeing someone so close to Bobby made me want to throw up. Much of my relationship with him was documented in *Confessions,* and I had not seen or heard from Bobby since the day I walked out on him in early 2003.

"Have you seen Bobby lately?" the friend asked.

"Where would I have seen Bobby?"

"I don't know, around L.A. somewhere?"

"No. Bobby and I don't run in the same circles."

"Oh, well, I just figured you might have seen him since he moved here, 'cause you know he and Whitney are getting divorced."

"Still? Well, no. I have not seen him, but tell him I said hello."

"Do you want to see him?"

"Hell, no!"

And there you have it, the easiest decision ever made. Didn't have to think twice. It was like dodging a bullet—a very large, very slow bullet, but one that I knew would ricochet back. And it did.

In *Confessions* I detailed my relationship with Bobby and its subsequent end, seemingly for good. For six months, from October 2002 through April 2003, he and I had carried on a tumultuous affair while he and his wife, Whitney Houston, were separated. Our relationship was filled with wild nights and comatose mornings, as I did my best to contend with his bad-boy impulses while trying to draw out the good man who lived within him. It was all to no avail. Soon I was exhausted from the constant pushing and pulling that defined our relationship. He and his wife reconnected, heading off to their now infamous, well-publicized trip to Jerusalem.

After I left, I never saw or spoke to him again. I didn't even say good-bye. I just walked away and that was it. Which meant there was no closure. We never discussed what went wrong in our relationship. I just left. For the next three years, I would neither see him nor hear from him, and that was fine by me.

Throughout our three-year hiatus, however, I'd always thought about him and kept my memories of him close to my heart, regarding him as one of the most special loves of my life. I know it sounds idiotic to the outsider who only knows him from what they have read or seen on television, but Bobby can be one of the warmest, most beautiful people on earth. He is also one of the most out-of-control men I have ever known.

To be completely honest, from the moment I first met Bobby Brown, I adored him, and after spending days and months on end with the self-proclaimed bad boy, I began to love him deeply. More than four years later, those sentiments remain, and amid all the tabloid rumors and questions, I find it imperative to supply answers and insight into my life with Bobby.

Bobby and I came face to face for the first time in three years on July 2, 2006, during the Essence Music Festival in Houston, Texas. After being enticed to a New Edition concert by Essence staff members trying to show me a good time, I stood in the wings, watching as Bobby prepared to perform. He danced around, shadow boxing and riffing as I stood still, frozen with fear and anxiety and overcome with familiar emotions.

Though we had been apart for three years, I knew at that exact moment that the way I felt for him back then was real, because here it was again. I loved him as if he'd never left. Our eyes eventually met, and as he walked toward me I didn't know whether to stay still and receive him, or run away. Indecisive, I stood there wondering what he would do and say. I breathed a sigh of relief as he embraced me, and held on for several seconds as I whispered, "I love you," and he returned, "I love you, too."

It's not easy to explain the sort of love Bobby and I shared then and do now. It is not by any stretch a romantic love but a comradeship, an understanding of confused souls. Bobby and I are two people who have been labeled and misjudged. We understand each other's tears, and we both fight to stay above water emotionally. I'm not sure I have ever known someone so well—not because he has told me who he is, but because I see pieces of my former self in him. I see a man who walks the earth in pain, and his only comfort is putting on a show, whether he's onstage or not.

Regardless of the differences he and I faced in our past relationship, seeing him again in Texas solidified for me that we would never really be apart, not even during our absences from each other. I held on to him as long as I could before it was time for him to hit the stage. As the crowd roared, tears streamed from my smiling eyes, knowing how much that roar meant to him. But as the performance went on and his showmanship heightened, my tears changed from pride to sadness. As he peeled away the layers of clothes he wore that night, he wound up standing there in slacks and an undershirt, sweat dripping from his swollen body. His stomach hung over his belt, and I saw members of the crowd cringe. I stood backstage feeling sorry for Bobby, knowing that this was all he ever wanted but that he wasn't the same. Those of us who love him keep the images of him at his best in our memories. Unfortunately, those days may be gone forever.

After the show, Bobby and I stood backstage talking, holding each other close. He told me he'd be in Los Angeles a couple weeks later. The thought of being with him again excited me. After Bill and I broke up the January before, life for me became business as usual. There was very little excitement in my personal life, and I found myself thirsting for pieces of my past. Not the sex, not the drugs, but the long nights in smoky pool halls playing pickups or greeting the sun from the balcony of a Beverly Hills hotel room where the rose champagne flows freely and room service is ultra-accommodating. I even missed the thrills of speeding along the Malibu coastline or down Sunset Plaza, smoking cigarettes in excess and sleeping until the afternoon. With Bill, everything was so wonderful but safe. With Bobby, I knew it wouldn't be either of the two, but I was ready for it—hell, I was begging for it. I needed the excitement. That night in Texas, as I walked away from him I whispered to myself, "I'm in trouble."

On July 15, 2006, New Edition and Bobby performed at the Greek Theatre in Los Angeles, and I was there to cheer on the group and reconnect with Bobby. I have a long-standing relationship not just with Bobby but with the other members of the band as well—Ricky, Johnny, and Ronnie, whom I dated briefly. I have known Ronnie since I first arrived in Los Angeles and he introduced me to Ricky back in 2000. Johnny and I first met at the home of Eddie Murphy, Easter 2003, and since then we have all remained social, seeing each other here and there. On this night, I stood just off the side of the stage as Bobby performed. I am always moved by his dedication to pleasing his audience, and this night was no different. His performance was better than the one in Texas, and I was moved to tears once again. At one point during the show he looked at me standing in the wings, winked, and nodded his head, acknowledging my presence. I was so very proud of him then, as I am now, and can only wish him the very best of everything. From that night forward, Bobby and I would reconnect in ways we never had before.

That first night together was exciting—staying up all night drinking, talking, and reminiscing. We stopped at a gas station somewhere near the Greek Theatre because I had to use the restroom, but the attendant wouldn't give us the key, presumably because it was well after two in the morning and he would have had to unlock the door to hand it to us, and we did come off a bit unruly. Still, my need was urgent, so Bobby and I went to the far corner of the parking area. I squatted down while he shielded me from view with his body. As I was squatting there I thought to myself, "If I was with Bill, he would never allow me to pee in a parking lot. He would make me wait till we found the nearest fancy restaurant, and then we'd have to order some wine before we left. You know, as déclassé as this is, it's a breath of fresh air."

That moment signifies our whole relationship. Bob is a person you could tell anything to, and he knows what you're talking about because he's done it. There's something very endearing about being with someone who allows you not to be perfect. With Bobby I knew

I could put my feet on the coffee table or belch really loud—he's a guy who will let you just be yourself. And at a time when I was being bashed for being myself, he was the only person I felt safe around, because he understood what it's like when being yourself gets you in a lot of trouble. He loves me for who I am, and that's why I love him to this day.

According to published accounts, Bobby and I lived together from July 2006 through early 2007. The truth is that Bobby was a part of my home, but strictly as a visitor, and only between July and October 2006. Why did I let Bobby Brown back into my life? My biggest fault in life is that I'm a nurturer. I take in everyone, which is why I'm always getting my feelings hurt.

At first he was a joy to have. We had drinks together, dinner together. When all is right with Bobby, he's nothing less than love-able. I knew I could walk into my house every day and know that he wasn't judging me or thinking bad things about me. He would wake up in the morning and make breakfast for everyone, singing and dancing all morning. At eight in the morning on weekdays he would take my son to school, making sure he was dressed, fed, happy, and equipped with last night's homework. Bobby never shied away from housework when he was at his best. We would spend days shopping for the week's dinner menu, and it was always a delight to see him in the kitchen making his famous fried chicken or fish. During these perfect moments, he was funny and amiable.

Nevertheless, although I cherished these times, I knew that the Mr. Hyde to his Dr. Jekyll was never far behind. It was one of those times when he was going to stay for a day, ended up staying for a week, and then was in the guest room for three months.

He wasn't here all the time. He would disappear for weeks on end, and then he would show up with his entire family. He had no place to live in Los Angeles, but he had his kids come to visit him at my house. His brother, Tommy, even had *his* kids come out to visit him, and so did their father. They were like nomads, and I was the safe haven. I was running a hotel—at one point there were nine people sleeping on my floor and in my guest room. At first I really enjoyed having the company. I love his family—they're funny and a lot of fun to be around. They love my son. But enough is enough after a while—thanks for visiting, but good-bye.

As I explained to Bill, Bobby and I were never with each other so much as we were simply around each other. I don't expect people to believe me, but Bobby and I never had sex when he was here. Our relationship had changed. He was dating someone else. He was here because there was nowhere else he could go where he could be taken care of. He didn't have any money. His girlfriend didn't have any money. We shared time and space on and off for several months, but he was never my boyfriend, we never lived together, and we were never expecting a child.

Bobby came to me with little or no money, no place of his own to sleep, and with the dissolution of his marriage weighing heavily on his shoulders. While his wife lived comfortably in Orange County with their daughter and continued to get her life and her sobriety under control, Bobby slept in my guest room, drinking and smoking his days away. There were days he didn't get out of bed, and those were the days I knew he was depressed. Then, all of a sudden, he would snap out of it and head to the kitchen to cook, with a song on his lips and a dance lifting his feet. Those days, I knew, were soon fleeting. Then there were the days when no one knew where Bobby was. He would spend weeks away, and those were the days I knew he was using. I always worried about him on those days, about where he was and if he was safe. I pictured him passed out on the floor of some stranger's filthy apartment, drunk and high, incapacitated, and unaware of the life he could be living. Any time he got a check in his hands, usually from performing, he would disappear and I wouldn't see him again until the money ran out.

Though our relationship is and always has been intense, it was not and is not a sexually charged one. The truth is that he could be a wonderful, passionate lover when times were good and he was sober. But when he was stoned and drunk—which was way too often—he had erection issues. I supported him in every way I could, including financially, always remembering the times he was there for me in the very same way. Three years earlier, when I had nothing, he gave to my son and me, and it was my privilege and good karma duty to give back and do the same for him when he needed my help. My love for him grew over the months as our relationship became more grounded yet, eventually, increasingly unstable.

Much of the world has speculated about Bobby's behavior and habits. What I know for sure is that his behavior is erratic at times and his habits are overwhelming—and possibly deadly. Just as in *Confessions,* I cannot say exactly what I have seen, but I know that Bobby needs help. My biggest fear for him was that I would walk into his room one morning and find that his heart had given out on him.

The situation only got worse; I was with him when he got served his papers, and it was all downhill from there. Between the pain of slowly losing his marriage and the effects of drugs and alcohol, I never knew whether he would make it through some of the roughest times, or even the night. Ricky, Johnny, and I would have long talks about how worried everyone was about Bobby and his fate, personally and professionally. We still do. I found, through his group members, that these men are a lot more than a finely tuned concert attraction. They are a brotherhood, and every single one of his brothers loves and fears for Bobby Brown.

CHAPTER NINE

Old Habits Die Hard

omantically, the year 2006 began disastrously with the notorious breakup between satirist Bill Maher and me on January 10. What the rest of the world doesn't know is that three days after our split, I suffered an emotional breakdown and was sent to the hospital for psychiatric observation. I cut my wrists and started drinking myself into an emotional tailspin. By the end of the night, not only were my faith in love and the love of my life gone, but also my son. Since Naiim and I have no family in California and his father abandoned him shortly after he was born, my son was picked up by child welfare services and made a ward of the state.

To explain: I have a history of chronic nervous breakdowns. I have them all the time. I also have a history of self-cutting. My psychologist tells me that it is not unusual for people who have been sexually abused in their youth to have a self-mutilation syndrome like cutting. Cutting is a way of releasing my pain, getting it outside me. When something is ailing me emotionally, I cut myself. I don't do it deeply, just enough to bleed. It calms me right away. Of course, it is a temporary fix.

I had a bad reaction to our breakup and cut my wrists. I was admitted to the hospital for observation. I suppose that it looked really bad to someone seeing this for the first time, but to me it was a usual occurrence, cutting myself for effect and not to commit suicide. The hospital psychologist explained to me that if they determined that I was mentally unstable, I would be held in a psychiatric ward for three days. That sobered me up quickly, because I worried immediately about my son, Naiim. I explained that I was under the regular care of a psychologist and had been diagnosed with a general anxiety disorder and a history of cutting. On top of that, I had had a bad night. Five or six hours later, I was released. Unfortunately, before I was released, a social worker came in and told me that my son had been taken into foster care.

For the next two weeks, I fought vigorously to put my life back together, knowing that the first step was to bring Naiim home. I went instantly into survival mode. When the shit hits the fan, I'm the girl you want. In a strange twist of fate, having my son ripped from my home was a blessing. I was forced to get over myself and my breakup with Bill and to focus on the one thing I should have been focused on all along: my son. There were court dates coming up in which I had to prove my competency as a mother, and I worked diligently to pull all my resources together.

My first step was to hire a Family Court–approved attorney with an impeccable reputation. In my search for such an attorney, I found out that I have a cousin in California who works for Family Court, who was able to tell me what to expect on entering the courtroom. Because of that information, I was sure to enroll in parenting classes and hire a court-accepted forensic physiologist before my first court date. What a blessing. Next, I had to have my mother come out to Los Angeles, knowing that the court would ask about next of kin. Though I have never been fond of my mother or ever bonded with her, it was imperative that we put our differences aside for my son's sake. At such a time, that was easy to do. I then called all my friends and asked each of them to write a character reference on my behalf for the judge. By time I saw the judge a week later, I was able to present her with over ninety letters and proof I was proactive in my case.

I was given the number to the foster home where Naiim was placed. The foster mom usually didn't allow parents to come to the home; you'd have to meet at a McDonald's or some neutral place, with someone watching you. Usually visits are only two or three hours twice a week, but she let me stay at the house all day, every day. Despite her good heart, the conditions in her home were deplorable. The home was cluttered and unkempt, with an occasional roach scuttling across the kitchen floor. Each time I visited, I brought home-cooked food for my son, because all she was giving the kids was ramen noodles with ketchup. What upset me the most is that my beautiful boy was made to spend his eighth birthday in a foster home. Though his grandmother and I brought him a cake and juice, sang the birthday song and bought him presents, nothing I could do, short of bringing him home, could make it right. I felt like a failure. Nothing mattered anymore. I knew I had to make my life right for my son, once again.

I had failed him and nearly destroyed our lives because I could not control the impulses of love and loss. I have spent all my life looking for my Daddy, and when Bill, whom I affectionately call "Daddy," left, I felt as if he had died. I was afraid I would never again be loved. Bill has always been so protective of me, always telling me the right things to do and say. He has always tried to help me be a better me, and in my stubbornness I was never willing to accept his gestures. Bill, I know for sure, loves me unconditionally. These days I am petrified of emotional commitment and stay clear of falling in too deep for anyone, even my Daddy. I never want to lose control again, but I am not sure I can maintain control *and* be in love. So I have turned my focus from my quest for love to the journey of life that Naiim and I have embarked on together.

For the first two weeks after Naiim was taken, I did everything I could to speed up the legal process and get him home. All of a sudden, nothing else in life mattered, and I was so grateful that God allowed me the financial resources to be able to take care of everything. Getting my son back quickly was expensive—I had to pay for parenting classes and attorney's and psychologist's fees. If I'd had to depend on the state to supply those services when it was convenient for them, it would have taken much longer to get my son back home with me.

Usually, if people can't afford the court-mandated steps, they have to file paperwork so the court can assign financial aid. This takes months. Meanwhile, they are shuffling your child around from one foster home to the next. I thank God I had the resources necessary to bypass the state's red tape. *Confessions,* for which so many condemned me, saved me and my son. Exactly fourteen days after he was sent to a foster home, Naiim was back in my arms, and my outlook on love and life changed forever.

Being loved is an amazing gift from God, and this is why he allowed me my son. No one in life will ever love me more than he does. But I believe I was also given the opportunity to be loved by another, who was not born of me but who chooses to stay with me and promises to do so all the days of my life. Bill is that blessing, and I could not—nor would I ever—ask for a better friend. Being loved and feeling loved counts for more than all the money and fame in the world. I often said, if given a choice, I would give all this up to be loved by that man and my little boy. Luckily, I don't have to choose. I can have it all.

There are details about my relationship with Bill that I will never be comfortable exploring in a public forum—not even the good times, which were many. I don't want to cheapen our relationship by trying to sum it all up in a chapter. What we have had and what we have now is bigger than this book. Of all my relationships, this one deserves to be protected.

That said, there are some bits about my relationship with Bill that I am happy to share. We met on April 20, 2005, at a party for *Smooth* magazine. It was the end of the party, and we were at a Hollywood club that had two levels with a back stairway that overlooked a back-yard patio. I was down on the patio, and I saw him up on the second level. I don't think I knew who he was; I know I hadn't watched his show. But I liked what I saw, and went charging up the stairs. That night a camera crew was following me around, capturing personal archives, and they caught our first meeting on video.

Bill and I are obviously very different people. He is nearly twice my age and extremely politically conscious, and as a Cornell gradu-ate, he can be quite the intellectual snob. However, despite our dif-ferences, we connected on a higher plane, doing and saying things with and for each other we never had before done or said with past loves. Publicly, he has been known to date women who tend to be porn stars, strippers, playmates, and the like. At first, I think, Bill thought I must have fit somewhere into that category. Though I have been two out of the three, I was on the verge of becoming a *New York Times* best-selling author and in need of my own identity.

Once my book was published and quickly becoming a success, I craved independence. Bill had always been outspoken about his dis-like of monogamy, but he was monogamous with me. We had a very committed relationship, and though it was what I wanted at first, it quickly became too much to bear. Bill and I soon began spending too much time together; he was so faithful, devoted, and attentive that he and our relationship began smothering me. I wanted to be more than just Bill Maher's girlfriend. I wanted to be who I was: Karrine Steffans, best-selling author.

Since we separated, he has continued to be a big part of my life.

We exchange the most hilarious, witty e-mails and phone calls. Once he sent me a note saying "Keep your nose to the grindstone— whatever that is!" So I found a picture on Google of a man putting his nose on a grindstone. Maybe you had to be there, but we're still laughing about that one. We're really becoming closer friends than we were before, and I prefer us as friends than as a couple, to my surprise.

All that is important is that I have loved him since the day we met and that as sure as the sun shines, he loves me and we have a bond not many can understand. As he says, he is the F. Scott to my Zelda, the Daddy to the little girl inside of me and the keeper of my heart. I don't know where we will be as our lives continue to take different paths, but I know one thing for sure: no matter where we go and whom we are with, we are always together.

It seems as though I would have learned the rules of engagement years ago, but old habits die hard and my quest for love has landed me in hot water more times than I care to admit. This time, however, I wasn't just in it but under it, and saw my life flash before my eyes as I drowned in my mistakes. During the healing process I clung closer to my son and began to see the straight and narrow path toward my next set of goals. Getting over Bill was hard, but getting over myself long enough to see the damage I was doing to my life and my son's life was even harder. I did it all in the name of love, which has nothing to do with love at all. Once my life became more stable, I swore off being in love and began enjoying my life as a single woman and mother to the most amazing young man I have ever met.

After a moment of seclusion, I felt well enough to stick my little toe into the casual dating pool, which landed me back in the arms of Ray J. It seems like a lifetime ago when I fell in love with Ray J. I was twenty-one, and he was just eighteen. I was running from my past, and he was young and looking forward to his future. I wrote about Ray J, the younger brother of singer Brandy, in *Confessions*, never thinking that he and I would touch souls again. But we have, and the experience has left me with unresolved feelings of what my life was, is, and can be.

Ray and I found ourselves together in early 2006, just after my split from Bill. With his then current relationship with Kim Kardashian on the rocks, and mine with Bill in the toilet, the connection we once had was nonexistent. We chalked up the time spent as just time in the company of a familiar friend; like slipping your foot in an old shoe. It had been years since we had seen each other, and found ourselves in a hotel room just looking at each other, catching up on the years past. We drank away our sorrows and fell asleep on each other, two broken spirits looking for comfort. Months later, we came together again, if just for a brief moment. We reconnected as we slow-danced to love songs at L'Ermitage Hotel in Beverly Hills in early October 2006. It felt better than an old shoe this time— it felt safe.

Being with Ray J that night reminded me of just a few of the things I had been missing with Bobby in residence. I felt pretty and young when Ray looked at me, the same way I feel when I am on my own. Whoever I spend time with shouldn't make me feel worse than I do when I am by myself—this I know, though I am not interested in falling in love after my last go at it ended so traumatically. I would still like to find someone who will slow-dance with me while overlooking the Beverly Hills skyline, for no reason at all. Ray was just as much an old habit as Bobby was, but one was no healthier than the other; each was unavailable in his own way. Still, it was nice for that night to slow-dance with an old friend and feel alive again, even if just for a moment. I knew that night that Bobby's days were numbered, and even though Ray was the one holding me, I knew that his number would also be up. We were too wounded, too affected, to go on.

After tossing the differences between them around in my head,

I have come up with this: no man is better than the other; they are just different. Everyone has faults and will let you down in some way, at some point. But some letdowns are easier to take and less malicious than others.

All of this makes me think of what Bill and I had, and I know now more than ever that he was the closest thing to "better" that I have ever found. I was happy with him, but it was the unhappiness with the direction of our relationship and with myself that drove a wedge between us. Not a day passed that I didn't know he loved me and put me first in all he did. I was never neglected; I was never forgotten. Unfortunately, because of Bill's feelings toward children, my son was. Bill tried to participate in Naiim's life, but we were never a unit, and that hurt.

As I run it all through my head and try to give these relationships some sort of rhyme or reason, I can't. I wish I could take Ray's romance, Bill's dedication, and Bobby's paternal instincts and wrap them all, nice and neat, into just one man. One day I will have it all, and this passage will seem as if someone else were telling the story, and that day will make all this worth it. But until then, I will lead with my heart and use my experiences to change myself until I am steadfast enough never to settle for anything less than what I deserve. Like most of us, I find myself taking what I can get and hoping the tides will change—that my love is strong enough to make a man into what I need. Even as I write this, I know it's an impossible feat, but it's the little girl inside me who's still hoping against hope and banking on a fairy-tale ending.

My success has made it easier to move forward and to plan a life alone. However, I cannot pretend to be an emotionless android and claim that my career gives me complete satisfaction or that being a mother is all I need. The truth is, I want to go home to Bill at the end of this journey, but I want to go back smarter, happier, and more secure than I was before. We still share an incredible love and an endearing friendship that is paralleled by no other, but something tells me that going through the wringer with everyone else will only help me know exactly what I need and what I need to give to be with the one man who has ever really loved me and still does to this day. And if there is a next time for us, it will be for all of us: me, Bill, and Naiim.

CHAPTER TEN

How to Save a Life, Part Two

While the rest of the world continued guessing the nature of my relationship with Bobby, I was working hard to help him be happy, healthy, and sane. Anyone who knows us could tell you about the nights I cried wondering where he was, and the days I lay in bed praying for a solution to his problems. I was obsessed with helping him and determined to love him unconditionally. He is almost like family to me, but my love for him exists on so many different levels that it would prove futile to try to explain to the rest of the world.

At this time I was confused about what I wanted out of my personal life. I had Bobby frequenting my home, off and on, and though we didn't share a sexual relationship, we were tangled in a deep friendship that often bordered on deeply disturbing. He could be disappointing on so many occasions, but on others I'd feel cherished and irreplaceable in his life as his unwavering friend and supporter. The longer he was there, the more days there were when I'd wake with him sleeping in the room next to mine and wonder what the hell I was doing.

Every time I thought about letting him and all his bad habits go, I'd also think of the way he loved my son—the way Naiim lit up when he was around. They had a relationship all their own that had nothing to do with me. Of all the men I have known, no one had ever embraced Naiim in this way, not even Bill, so I held on to Bobby a little longer for these reasons, wondering if I was doing myself and my son an injustice in the long run. There are very few perks to our friendship, and it's always more of a hassle than a pleasure. But in the recesses of my mind it was the image of my son's bright smile when he heard this man walk through the front door. Yet, just as soon as he came in, he'd be gone again, chasing his habits. Bobby could never be tamed.

As we read the reports and gossip columns about our supposed romance, Bobby and I laughed at how much the world did not know. So much of it was incorrectly reported that we tried our best to stay out of the public eye and go about our lives as friends. We ate out often, went to clubs, barbecued by the pool, or lay around doing nothing at all. We shared secrets and even created a few along the way. As his divorce proceedings carried on, however, our relationship became increasingly strained and we grew apart slowly. It was becoming apparent to me that no matter what I did or said, I couldn't fix anything in Bobby's life. I even discussed conducting an intervention with his friends to help place him in a rehabilitation center, but even that plan fell apart as Bobby became unavailable to all who reached out to him.

One day in October 2006 it became evident that Bobby wanted to do it all on his own—and that he should. No one could help him do what he needed to do, and after a quick trip to Las Vegas, Bobby returned, determined to ruin our friendship and his own life. He was in Sin City to visit Mike Tyson, who had invited both of us to see him train. Knowing the two very well, I knew I would be out of place with them. Recently, the whole world found out about Mike what I have known for almost a decade—when the champ was arrested in

Phoenix, Arizona, for, among other things, possession of cocaine. Mike subsequently checked himself into a California rehabilitation facility. His arrest was a relief for me and for some of those closest to him, for it could be the beginning of a new life for the heavyweight.

It was in Phoenix that Mike and I met in 1999. I had recently separated from my son's father and was on my own for the first time. After being with the same man for four years from the age of seventeen, I was on the prowl, ready to date again. As I made my way around the city's most popular night club, I noticed that most everyone was moving toward the back of the venue and surrounding the VIP area. I made my way through the crowd to see what the big commotion was about, only to find Mike in the middle of it all. As I walked past his table and toward the restroom, I stared at him. He seemed larger than life to me, a figment of my imagination, but as his eyes locked with mine, he smiled, and the fictitious giant all of a sudden became real. He tapped a member of his entourage, whispered in his ear, and pointed to me; next thing I knew, I was being hoisted up to the VIP area and introduced to the man who would become one of my dearest friends and, years later, my most dangerous liaison.

Over the next several years, Mike and I would stay in touch over the telephone but never saw each other again until 2002, after I'd moved to Los Angeles. I had a friend who told me he was staying at the W Hotel in Westwood, just adjacent to Bel-Air. She said that she was going to see him. "Take me with you," I told her, "but don't tell him I'm coming."

He was shocked to see me. After the years that had passed, we were both extremely curious about the sexual tension between us, and finally gave in to our desires.

As long as I have known Mike, he has proved to be very passionate about everything and everyone in his life. He is a lover and a fighter, but he loves the same way he fights: hard and rough. His kisses are like uppercuts, and his lovemaking is like a title match. He pushed and pulled; he tossed me around like a rag doll. And just as he proved in June 1997 during his rematch with Evander Holyfield, Mike Tyson is a biter. His passion manifested through pain, and as I endured the extreme force of his two-hundred-pound frame colliding into mine, he kissed, sucked, and bit me overzealously.

I wanted nothing more than for him to stop. I was in excruciating pain as we continued in this manner for several hours. Finally, at the end of our first tryst, I was spent, and covered in bruises and bite marks. I vowed never to have sex with him again—it was just too brutal. "Honey," I said, "we're just going to be friends. This is ridiculous."

Mike is the type of man who does everything in excess, whether it's good or bad for him. He is a man with very few boundaries in his life. He searches for control over his life and his appetites, but is often unable to maintain it. When he and Bobby teamed up in Las Vegas, I expected nothing but trouble. I stayed behind and just prayed they'd both make it out of Vegas alive. They did, but none the better for the experience. When I picked Bobby up from the airport a few days later, he reeked of liquor. By the dilation of his eyes and his jerking body movements, I knew he was high. The ride home was quiet as my hands gripped the wheel and I fumed from within. He was disgusting, and though I didn't want him roaming the streets or sleeping in alleyways, I knew I couldn't have him in my home much longer. Once at home, I began to ride Bobby about his condition, and as usual, he took offense.

Of the all the things Bobby could have said to me, the one thing he shouldn't have said was "What have you done for me? You've never done shit for me!" I looked at him, standing in my home, wearing clothes and shoes I'd bought him, drinking liquor I supplied, in a glass I paid for. I couldn't believe he had the audacity to say what he had, drugs or no drugs. Ingratitude was the last straw.

It became apparent to me that I was slowly killing myself while trying to save a life. I wasn't able to eat or sleep regularly. I was often upset, crying and screaming at him in fits of rage, physically fighting him, kicking him out and letting him back in. I began to tell our friends, "This is not my life. This is Whitney's life—and I wish she would come get her life back." But in fact, this was Bobby's life, and he was dragging me down with him. Slowly but surely, I was drowning. All of a sudden, I realized that the life that needed saving was my own.

And there it was. It was either him or me. I had to jump ship. Based on my rude awakening, I had a major decision to make, but it was one I'd become very familiar with over the past several years of my life. I had defended him to everyone I knew, but there would be no gray area with Bobby, and I understood, as did many of his friends, that the best way to love him would be from a distance. It was early October when I asked Bobby to stop frequenting my home and to cut all communication with my son and me. Initially, the decision was tough on everyone, but over time Naiim and I grew accustomed to having our new house to ourselves for the first time since moving in.

There were days when I missed Bobby so much, I was moved to tears and fought the urge to call him and ask him to stop by. There were nights he'd call just to check on my son and ask how things were at the house. The truth was that with every passing day in the wake of his departure, my house was feeling more and more like a home—my home. I was finding my groove and a schedule that made life simpler than when Bobby was around. With him, life was chaotic; nothing was ever organized, and life's plans and schedules went out the window. He would sleep all day, stay awake all night, and fumble business meetings, missing some completely, throwing away opportunity at the drop of a hat. I was able to get interest for him from HarperCollins for a book deal, but he didn't show up to the meeting, because he was too drunk. When he started batting down things that would help him, I knew it was time for him to go.

I needed Bobby to leave, but he needed it just as badly. As he dealt with his life, I began dealing with mine. My new home needed my attention, and so did my son and career. When I sat back and looked at all I have accomplished in my life I realized how backward my thinking had been. Here I was giving so much time, energy, and support to someone whose most recent accomplishments paled in comparison to mine—instead of focusing on retaining my achievements and building on them. And though I could afford Bobby I couldn't afford to be around him. I often find that I want to give too much of myself—a self who is still underdeveloped and isn't finished setting anchors in the tide.

Bobby still calls periodically, and he has even dropped by the house to say hello or see my son. But it is different. He's in control. He knows that he has to be in control. I hope that we will always be friends—but never again the way we once were.

The best thing I ever did for my friend Bobby was to let him be, and give him the space he deserves to get it all back together again. The best thing he ever did for me was to allow me the opportunity to learn a difficult lesson. Sometimes love is not a two-way street. Sometimes there's just a one-way private road that leads to your own happily-ever-after, without anyone else along for the ride.

CHAPTER ELEVEN

Black Tie

On Friday, September 29, 2006, Earvin "Magic" Johnson celebrated his twenty-fifth year in business, with a black-tie gala at the Beverly Hills Hilton. Though Magic and I have been friends for over five years, I was not aware of the event until just a few days before. He and I are not in constant contact and tend to catch up every few months or so. Either way, I was excited to attend the soiree and to celebrate with Magic alongside his family, friends, and colleagues.

The day started with a frantic shopping spree as I raced around town running last-minute errands to prepare for the red carpet. Being an avid window shopper, I knew exactly where to go for a formal black gown that was not only elegant but also undeniably sexy and form fitting. So I made my way to Sunset Plaza, a trendy two-mile stretch of road on the west side of Los Angeles, just minutes from Bel-Air and Beverly Hills. Sunset Plaza is home to some of the most exclusive and pricy boutiques as well as an array of restaurants that not only serve the finest cuisine but also complement the posh Los Angeles lifestyle I have grown accustomed to, making the area one of the *it* places to see and be seen.

As I walked into BCBG Max Azria, my eyes were drawn to a rack of floor-sweeping black gowns in the far left corner of the room—and, just my luck, the entire selection was marked down. Within minutes I managed to find my size, try it on, fall in love with it, make the purchase, and walk out.

(I haven't yet arrived at the level in my career where I can call a stylist and have dresses brought to my home for selection. As nice as that would be, I am entirely capable of living my life without help every step of the way, and I never want to fall into the habit of needing others to perform the simplest tasks. I still shop at the mall and buy off the rack, and I am always intrigued by a sale.)

Luckily for me, I was able to walk out of BCBG with the perfect gown for less than sticker price, and with time to spare. With the wind at my heels, I headed over Coldwater Canyon, leaving the West Side and heading into the San Fernando Valley to make a drastic change—a haircut. I headed to the salon and asked my favorite stylist to chop off my long hair.

With a fabulous dress and a fresh bob, I threw myself together for Magic Johnson's event. A publicist for the event had called while I was at BCBG, to confirm my impeding arrival. An hour later she called me back.

"Karrine, Mr. Johnson wanted me to confirm that your guest for the evening will be Bobby Brown."

"Who? No—what are you talking about?"

"Oh, well, then, I'm sorry, but we won't be able to accommodate you for the evening. You see, Mr. Johnson gave you someone else's seats, based on Bobby Brown's celebrity and the relationship that he has with Mr. Johnson."

I was pissed. "First of all," I told her, "let's be honest. I am a bigger celebrity than Bobby Brown right now. Secondly, he and Mr. Johnson *have* no relationship. I am attending the event based on my relationship with Mr. Johnson, and on that premise alone. So you do what you need to do, and you tell Mr. Johnson I will speak with him about this later."

For those of you who may be unaware, Magic Johnson has been a pivotal part of my life since the year 2001. I was dead broke and homeless, living out of my car with Naiim, who was three at the time, when he and I met. On my being introduced to Earvin, he instantly took responsibility for my son and me and made sure we had food and a place to stay. Since that time, Magic has celebrated my accomplishments every step of the way, and with each bit of progress he has been there with a bouquet of roses, a warm smile, and heartfelt congratulations on my success.

What this publicity bitch was trying to tell me made no sense. If Magic had been my champion all these years why would he suddenly say that I could attend his event only if I was with Bobby Brown, of all people? I mean, really—come on! After all Earvin had done for me and meant to me, was I supposed to believe this was true? No.

Immediately I called Earvin. He denounced the publicist and said, "Of course you can come. I wouldn't have it any other way." Within minutes, she called me back, claiming to have miraculously found an open seat.

What am I, an idiot? This is what I know for sure: there are people who don't know who I am, and there are those who don't know who *I* am. Confusing? Let me explain.

Some have never heard of me, and I love that—the anonymity of it all. Then, there are those who know my name, know my face, have read or heard of *Confessions of a Video Vixen* and think they have me pegged. So they assume that I am a different person from who I am in reality. Anyone who would imply that I have to be invited to events under someone else's name is quite mistaken. I have worked long and hard to earn my own notoriety and social standing, and I don't need to be on the arm of any man to go anywhere or do anything. Those days are over for me; I do not need to be attached to someone else for validation.

When I wrote *Confessions,* it changed the way influential people in the industry saw and treated me. Whether they loved or hated the book, they respected me for it. Very few women in my demographic have the opportunity to explore their innermost thoughts, mistakes and all, and turn them into a best-selling book. Very few of us will ever have the chance to mold our culture. People in powerful positions want me around—they don't try to keep me out of black-tie galas. So after the publicist working the event was properly scolded, I went to the party, secure in my friendship with Magic Johnson and the fact that I belonged there with or without Bobby Brown—or anyone else, for that matter.

I laughed on the inside as I greeted the publicist at the red carpet and she had to watch me walk the walk with cameras flashing and paparazzi screaming my name, vying for my attention. She, like many, had me pegged all wrong. I worked the carpet, and it was a glorious moment being out there alone, making my own name in the world. I have to admit, I absolutely loved it!

As I walked the red carpet, I stopped for a few minutes to chat with Shaun Robinson from *Access Hollywood.* Then I skipped the second half of the carpet to hurry into the green room before the seven o'clock dinner began. While standing around waiting for my photo opportunity with Earvin, I heard a voice from behind saying, "That's a bad bitch." I turned around to see former NBA star Dennis Rodman standing behind me.

"Are you talking to me?" I replied with a coy, shy smile. He instantly engaged me in conversation and intrigued me not only with his bizarre physical appearance but with his off-putting attitude. Dennis is a legend, and though he has shown great skill in the sport of basketball, I believe he has become associated primarily with tasteless scandal—from random acts of cross-dressing to marrying himself.

Either way, I was intrigued and wanted to know more. After all I had heard about Dennis, I wanted to form an opinion of my own. I wondered if he was really as crazy as everyone around town said, and if he and I could be friends. Shortly after our initial conversation, I accompanied Dennis to his table and spent the next thirty-five minutes with him. I have to admit, by the end of our time together, I had a headache and was looking for a way out. Although I find it easier to socialize with people in the artistic community, such as fellow authors, actors, directors, network executives, and the like, I also run the risk of meeting some of the strangest individuals walking the planet. The spotlight changes everyone. Some become humble and buy property in Ohio and Louisiana to escape Hollywood's glare. Some are drawn to it like moths to a flame, except that when they are burned they continue to hover around it, wounded.

For the entire time he and I sat together, Dennis had nothing to say that was pleasant or progressive. It was "I hate this and I hate that." "This sucks and that sucks." He told me that he was actually in the mood to wear a dress instead of the dress shirt, jacket, and jeans that he wore to the gala. In fact, he looked very presentable that night, and I was impressed by how well he cleaned up. He said that his manager, who was with him, insisted that he dress appropriately, though he would have preferred to show up in a gown. He said he hated the atmosphere: the crowd of businesspeople, media, and celebrities; the formality of it all; and the ever-popular Hollywood schmooze—the hugging and kissing, the "let's get together" and "call me" promises of the evening.

I've always thrived in these settings, but I would have to agree with Dennis that he most certainly didn't fit in with the mainstream crowd. By the end of our conversation, I came to several conclusions, the most important being that this man is an absolute nut. It became evident to me that he is an example of what happens when you hit the top and then slam headfirst to the bottom. He was bitter, he was angry, and I was ready to go.

He invited me out with him and his friends for sushi, and I quickly refused, saying I had come with someone who needed me to drive him back home. Dennis's response was, "So what?" That seemed to be his attitude about everything, and yet, even though he was so set against the public and the publicity machine that is Hollywood, he also seemed to want a way in. In addition to his initial plan to wear a gown to Magic's event, which would no doubt have caused a media frenzy, he also discussed his plans to travel to New York City's Times Square and drop one million dollars in cash from the roof of a building. This was yet another scheme to draw attention to himself. So one must wonder, if someone is so set against Hollywood, then why would he want to draw closer to it? Why would Dennis claim to be so uncomfortable in the spotlight, yet wave his hands in desperation for the lights to find him?

Celebrity is addicting and its withdrawal is sometimes unbearable. Like a heroin addict, you express disdain for the drug, and after your first hit you can't function without it. When it leaves you, it's prone to make your body shake and leave your pillow soaked from nightmare-induced cold sweats. You fear never being celebrated again and that you'll never be as high as you were before. Unlike heroin, there is no substitute to wean you from celebrity. There is no methadone that can take the place of the flashbulbs of the paparazzi, the signing autographs on restaurant napkins, or being part of the number one team in the NBA and being celebrated by the world. There is no substitute for being ranked the best.

With my head spinning, I excused myself from the table, but not before Dennis gave me his phone number. I promised to call later that evening but couldn't bring myself to do so. The night was going too well to have my spirits brought down by his ranting. But I have to admit, I am still intrigued, not so much by him but by the culture of celebrity that I find myself tossed into. The way I figure it, if I pay attention, I can learn from the mistakes of others just as quickly as from the achievements of others.

In the room that night were some of the most noteworthy people in business and government, and they were all there to celebrate my friend Magic Johnson. All he has achieved inspires me, and for the first time since I have known him, at this gala I began to see how he functions in the bigger picture. Earvin leads by example and has learned not only to multiply his business ventures, one leading seamlessly into another, but how to teach young men and women the essentials of business and personal strength. He is the sort of man who, when he speaks, always gives something to learn from. He has expanded my knowledge of financial planning and stability, product placement and joint ventures, and even—especially—the importance of relationships in this town and this industry.

No question, Magic Johnson has been a positive influence in my life and my son's life for years. Then, sitting next to me, was the opposite portrayal of an NBA personality. After speaking with Dennis Rodman, I was exhausted. His energy and ideas are draining, to say the least. His attitude is the sign of a man unfulfilled and struggling to stay afloat in the sea of public attention and notoriety. With no humility, poise, or grace, he is the epitome of a man who has been chewed up and spit out. There before me were two sides of the same coin, and I knew just what to do. While looking up and forward, I must also look down and behind at those who have not achieved their full potential for greatness. There is a lot to learn from both.

Chapter Twelve

Mother, May I?

Growing up, I had dreams—and not just your average, run-of-the-mill ballerina dreams. No, I wanted to be a rich and famous writer. I wanted the world to know my pain. I wanted to release it into the universe and let it come back to me clean. I listened to Sheila E.'s *Glamorous Life* and Tracy Chapman's *Fast Car* and daydreamed about being someone different from who I was. From the time I was five, I remember being praised and rewarded for my writing by local government officials and pillars of the community. I remember my grandmother being there for me with a new dress and shiny new patent leather shoes every time I performed something I had written. I remember her cheering for me and supporting my dreams, letting me know that what I wanted was not just plausible but inevitable. I have no such memories of my mother. None.

Now, twenty-five years later, how am I supposed to find closure with my mother? How am I supposed to forget, forgive, or move away from the feelings I owned then? Am I not supposed to own them now, because my body is bigger? The truth is that no matter how many years have passed, no matter where I go or what I do,

I will always be that little girl looking into the crowd for her mother and coming up empty.

It is a fact that the most formative years in a person's life are between birth and five years old. According to my psychologist, the years between five and twelve are also very crucial, and both these times lay the foundation for who someone will be as an adult. I know that many people can never understand the possibility of not loving your mother as a mother or respecting her as a person. Trust me, it's hard to explain, but I will try. If the ages between birth and twelve are the most formative and you give a child some of the most undeniably miserable moments and memories of her life, then wouldn't you expect that to stick with her just as easily as the lesson that one plus one is two?

I learned a lot of things from my mother during my years living with her, and some of them were necessary, positive lessons. Those have stuck with me as well: how to keep a clean house and how to cook for my family. I learned from my grandmother about discipline, and I carry those old-school principles with me and have raised my son successfully with them. I have carried the negative into adulthood, but I have also carried countless useful and positively balancing experiences. As I tell those friends closest to me, it's not as if my mother and I had a falling-out just a few years ago and I refuse to grow up and away from it. The feelings I have are deep-rooted, and I do not expect them to change, nor do I want them to change. However, please understand that my animosity toward my mother and the time we spent together throughout my childhood does not keep me from sharing telephone conversations with her, or even time at my Los Angeles residence. I do not allow our strained relationship to bleed into the one she has with my son, who adores her.

I have the ability to own my feelings, not sugarcoat them, to live with and accept them and then incorporate them into my life. I accept those emotions just as they are, without feeling the need to change them and make things better. If I don't like you, it's okay, and if the feeling is mutual, that's even better. In my opinion, life is too short to put energy into changing the things that are meant to be. Besides, as the saying goes, you can't put the toothpaste back in the tube.

With my feelings toward my mother set in stone, I am careful and ever vigilant about the ways in which I love my son. As a single mother, I walk a fine line every day between strictly disciplining my son and tenderly loving him. At nine years old, he is still my baby. Actually, he is growing up right before my eyes and turning into a young man with hints and promises of the grown man he will one day be. And though I have failed at times, as all mothers do, I am confident that I am raising him well and giving him a life he can be proud of. I am careful to be honest with him and allow him to voice his opinions, which I always take into account.

As a young girl, I never felt as if my emotions or opinions mattered to my mother. It was always, "I'm the mother and you're the child. Don't ask me any questions and stay in a child's place." Children tend to be more honest and, many times, smarter than the adults who raise them. Children are not jaded and ruined by the world around them. They do not see the world through rose-colored glasses or make up scenarios in their heads to feel better about themselves or the lives they lead. Children see things just as they are, and call it as they see it.

Because children see the world without filters, it is important for me to listen to my son and make his opinions matter. He is actually helping me to stay grounded when I see the world through his eyes. What I try to do is take the examples of my upbringing, repeat the good ones, reverse the bad ones, and try not to be too hard on myself when I make mistakes. Most of all, I have learned to accept the way things are between my mother and me, without longing to have them change.

I don't find it necessary to recount the mistakes of my past here on this page. *Confessions* explained them, and I have sent those thoughts and grievances into the universe, so they no longer weigh me down. What remains is only natural, and I know that I cannot change the past or make it better.

During my weekly sessions with my therapist, this was the breakthrough that put my entire life into perspective: I don't have to make it better. Finally, it's okay not to have to fix it. I have never felt freer than I do now, and this is not because I have moved past my personal history, but simply because I accept it. It has made me who I am, and even the most painful moments serve good deeds in my life today. I refuse to grow bitter and to let the weight of my youth and the mistakes of others, or myself, bury me before I am dead. Finally, I live.

CHAPTER THIRTEEN

God Bless the Child

My birthday present to myself in August 2006 was the purchase of my first home. The million-dollar property sits on a hillside, which I also own, and offers spacious living quarters and over twenty-three thousand square feet of land. For a first house, I did well, but I still look forward to the purchase of my next home, which will have to be bigger and better, naturally. That's always been one of my foibles—I have a hard time appreciating where I am and what I have, not because I am ungrateful but because I always want more.

After I moved into the house, I began making improvements to the property, one of which was security fencing around the perimeter. Suddenly I needed two remotes to get into my garage, one for the motorized entry gate, and the other for the garage itself. Between the two of them, I sometimes feel as if I am at a space vessel's control panel. One day during the first week of October, I turned into my driveway and clicked the gate remote. As it opened, I slowly pulled into my driveway, then clicked the garage remote—or what I *thought* was the garage remote.

Disaster followed. What I had clicked was not the garage remote but the gate remote, signaling it to close. As I was driving through the iron gate, it closed on my Mercedes Benz E350, scratching it from bumper to bumper. The car was virtually brand-new, and now there was a deep gouge that ran the length of the car. What I had done put me into a full-fledged panic attack. As far as I was concerned, the car was ruined, but what I did next made me seriously consider the changes my life has undergone and how I have dealt with them.

It was not so long ago that I received an e-mail from the publishing house HarperCollins and this amazing journey into prosperity began. It was January 2005 when I sat on the edge of my bed, checking my mail. On opening the message, I began to shake as it requested my speedy response to the question "Would you like to publish your memoirs?" The offer could not have come at a better time. I was flat broke, other than the five hundred dollars I had just borrowed from Mike Tyson the night before. In front of me was a lowball contract from some Hollywood creeps, practically asking me to sign my life away for the measly sum of five thousand dollars. The offer was pitiful, but I was considering it because I really needed the money. There was an eviction notice posted on my door. I knew that these small-time producers were looking to take advantage of me. They knew I was flat broke and unable to pay my rent or buy groceries without the help of friends like Mike Tyson.

I was contemplating it all when I got the message from Gilda at HarperCollins. That night I tore up their measly offer and left a message for Gilda to call me bright and early the next day. When she did, she set the wheels in motion for my first book deal, but the genesis of the book had happened the year before.

Confessions was originally the suggestion of André Harrell, a huge figure in the music and entertainment industry. It was a man who told me to do this. Every time he saw me he said, "Karrine, I'm not going to say anything to you except three words, 'Write the book.'" I saw him at brunch at the Four Seasons a few months later, and he wouldn't even talk to me. He just said, "Write the book," and went back to his food.

I knew that what he was saying was right. What dawned on me was that all these relationships that I had been getting all this heat for were still my relationships. I still had numbers of some of the most powerful people in the entertainment industry. Whether I had sex with them didn't matter. They were still my relationships. I started calling people I knew, either platonically or not, saying, "I have this idea. André says I should write this book, and I trust him, but common business sense tells me that people are interested in someone who other people are interested in."

There's a bandwagon in this business. No one is going to notice you until someone else notices you first. But once those wheels are set in motion and that wagon starts rolling, everyone's running as fast as they can because they're dying to jump on board. I knew that to get a good offer for a book, I had to draw attention to myself, and that meant launching my own little do-it-yourself publicity campaign. The way I decided to make noise was to get the two biggest magazines in this industry to run my story simultaneously. I called Shakim Compere, Queen Latifah's business partner and manager. Shakim called the editor of *Vibe* magazine and said, "Karrine has an incredible story. She's a friend of mine. It involves a lot of artists. Listen to her." *Vibe* did a six-page photo spread accompanied by an extensive article. Simultaneously, I received a call from a woman I'd met before who, at the time, was a writer for *XXL* magazine, *Vibe*'s direct competitor, who was interested in the same story. I couldn't turn down the opportunity to be featured in both magazines, at full capacity, at the same time, when actually no magazine wants to run the same story, at the same time, as its number one competitor. Instead, they want to one-up each other, which meant I now had to lie to both of them about what I was doing. *Vibe* called me and asked, "Are you doing something with *XXL*?"

"No."

XXL called. "Are you doing something with *Vibe*?"

"No." By the time they figured out that I had finagled the whole thing, it was too close to their publishing date for either of them to back out.

All through 2004, I was featured in ten magazines within twelve months, thanks to the favors of some of my closest friends in journalism. This was before a book deal was even on the horizon. Then I used my friends in the media to leak items about me in the press, like the now infamous story about my relationship with Usher. Little by little, I proved I was newsworthy by staying in the news. This is what prompted HarperCollins to ask me if I wanted to publish my memoirs.

That was January, and the book was to be published in June, which meant that it had to be finished by the end of March. Over the next three months, I worked diligently to complete and edit the manuscript that would become *Confessions of a Video Vixen*. I wrote it on an old computer with a dial-up modem, in sixty days. To send the manuscript that way took me all night. I'd hit the send button before I went to bed and then get up in the morning, hoping it had gone through.

That book was a new beginning for Naiim and me. It saved our lives. Before publishing the memoir, I wasn't able to support myself despite odd jobs here and there. Between my nearly two-thousand-dollar rent, five-hundred-dollar car payment for my 2001 Mercedes Benz C240, and child-care bills, times were tough. I always found myself living from moment to moment, or off the generosity of others. Everything I did was dependent on someone else's resources, their career, their willingness to lend a hand. I was unhappy with the way my life was, and worked hard to find a way out. After causing a flurry of media attention to myself for nearly a year before HarperCollins acknowledged me, I was relieved to have my efforts rewarded. I would never again be dependent, and from that day on I would be a better-prepared provider for my young son.

Soon came fancier cars and the purchase of my first home and, of course, the gate fiasco. It was eight thirty in the morning when the accident happened; by eight forty-five, I was on the road, headed to Mercedes Benz of Encino. While driving like a bat out of hell up Ventura Boulevard, I called the dealership, looking for the salesman who had sold me the car just six months before. He and I had kept in touch, and I found him to be both considerate and accommodating. The dealership's main switchboard operator answered the call. "Mercedes Benz of Encino. May I help you?"

"Hi, is Stephan in?"

"I'm sorry, Stephan is off today. May I transfer you to another of our associates?"

"No. I *need* Stephan," I said firmly. "Can you please call him on his mobile and connect us? Tell him Karrine is calling and it's an emergency."

"Would you like me to transfer you to the service department?"

"No! I want Stephan! I am on my way there and I have a Mercedes Benz emergency!"

"Do you need roadside assistance?"

"No! I need a new car!"

A pregnant pause hung in the air before she patched me through to Stephan's mobile phone. Within minutes I was at the dealership. Stephan was there to meet me, having canceled his doctor's appointment. There I was, screeching into the lot and barreling through the showroom like the diva of all divas when the truth is, I am not that way at all. In the land of divas I can't be considered anything but a lightweight—not when there are people like Madonna and Mariah Carey in the world. Even though my diva-dom pales in comparison to theirs, my lifestyle is still very new to me and is a big step away from where I was just a few years ago.

It took Stephan just a few minutes to find me a suitable replacement for my 2006 E350. He showed me a 2007 E550; I took one look at the car and asked Stephan to take the deal to Financing. The time I sat there waiting for them to crunch the numbers was just long enough for me to start thinking about what was really going on here. My head was pounding, and my heart raced with anxiety as I ran the facts through my head.

Just four years before, I was homeless and sleeping in a 1995 Nissan Maxima. Now here I was, having scratched my new Mercedes in an action that was nobody's fault but my own, running headlong to the dealership and demanding a newer, better one just minutes later. In short, I was behaving like a spoiled brat, a trust fund baby who was accustomed to indulging her every whim at a moment's notice. I wanted to cry as I wondered what had happened to me. I began to feel guilty and unworthy of all my good fortune and all the things I have been given.

Just then I watched a city bus drive past. I thought to myself that every last person on it would rather drive a scratched Mercedes than ride the bus, if given the choice. Just the fact that I have the ability to switch from one Benz to another made me want to vomit, especially when I realized that this was the third new one I'd purchased in just a couple of years! My first Mercedes was worth one year of my mother's salary; the second, two years; and the third, three. I could barely recognize the life I was living as my own, and wondered why I wasn't satisfied with a scratched Benz. Why couldn't I live with it for a day, or even just an hour or two?

When you begin to make more money than the people around you, they sometimes say, "The money has changed you." Those who have money tend to say, "The money hasn't changed me; it's changed those around me." Everyone is pointing the finger at others, and no one is taking responsibility.

I now find both statements true. My success has surely changed some of the people around me, and changed the way they respond to me. Whenever we did Sunday brunch or went shopping, they would become frustrated or even embittered because what should have been a pleasant experience brought home the gap between our finances in a really negative way. I don't like making people feel bad, so I try not to shop or eat extravagantly around friends who are not as well-to-do as I am.

Even more so, however, success has certainly changed me. I am not the person I was before *Confessions,* college lectures, and talk show appearances—and I am certainly not the same person I was before becoming financially stable. I have changed, and though it may seem subtle to some, it's a huge deal to me.

I drove away in my new Mercedes Benz and was headed to my neighborhood sushi restaurant with these thoughts resting heavily on my mind. I wondered if it would only get worse; this feeling of entitlement, this *I want what I want and I want it now* attitude. I try to maintain a sense of humility and strive daily never to forget where I came from, but on that October day, I felt I had. I had brought an acquaintance with me to the dealership, and as we left in the new car, he checked his e-mail and read me the latest hip-hop news. Rapper Cassidy (born Barry Reese) had been critically injured when a U-Haul swerved into his SUV, fracturing his skull. All of a sudden, my hissy fit seemed ridiculous and my blessings became apparent. On hearing the news, I asked my companion, "If I roll out of this parking lot in that new car, bitching about it, and a truck hits and kills me, will I be happy with the way I spent my last moments?" The answer to that question changed my day and all the days to follow.

In a life filled with red carpets and black-tie galas, it is sometimes difficult to stay grounded and live in the real world. It's important, however, as we go along in this city of broken dreams and misplaced promises, to watch for the signs. Signs and angels come in the most unassuming and unlikely shapes, and they can easily be missed. I have missed many signs in my life and have paid the consequences for my ignorance. God knows I still miss signs, but at least I am aware now that they exist. Based on my experiences and contrary to the old adage, ignorance is not bliss. When you feel yourself getting too full of yourself and too self-absorbed, be on the lookout. Chances are, the universe will be trying to tell you something, and you may not always like the way it chooses to deliver the message.

I was reminded that day to live life to its fullest, to treat myself and not be afraid to make my life what I want it to be. To fill my home with love and security and all the things that make it cozy, warm, and inviting. I soon bought yet another Mercedes. I had always wanted a convertible roadster to drive up the coast; I'd dreamed of it ever since I was a child. I was reminded to take time for myself, away from the phone calls and e-mails that invade my life. I spend long mornings and afternoons at the Four Seasons Hotel writing and sampling exotic foods and wines, learning more about them. Most important and enjoyable, I was reminded to continue spending time with my son, enjoying his hilarious sense of humor and view on life.

None of this is about the money; it's about taking what you have been given and making the very best of it. It's about remembering that life is short and that none of us knows when we'll be called to leave. We should make every moment count and strive for happiness any and every way we can. All our abilities are different, so find your own happiness according to how you live your life.

I have now been blessed with more that I need, and though there are days when living in excess is fun, there are more days when a trip to Baskin-Robbins and then to the park with my son is all I want. I never want to forget the days when we couldn't afford an ice-cream cone, much less a Mercedes Benz, and when the car was also our living space. Now every weekend there is a slumber party and cupcake bake at my house, and there is nothing that can replace the smile on my son's face as he proudly plays host to his friends in his new home.

For me, it's about building a complete life, a life where my son has access to the finer things but is taught to find joy in the simpler things as well. And though there are people in the world who have so much more materially than we do, many lack the happiness we've found. I will always be reminded of when my son and I had less of everything, and know that we have more than enough today. I have been reminded to go for what I want, and I have learned to be happy with all I have and to count nothing small.

CHAPTER FOURTEEN

Say Good Night

It never ceases to amaze me how some people can't seem to get over my past—the partying, the relationships, the sex, the thoughtlessly self-imposed nickname "Superhead." If I have been able to move forward, then why are so many people still stuck on my past, as if my life were theirs? It's not as if I were the only one living that lifestyle—lots of women are still doing that. The inevitable truth about life, especially life in our twenties, is that we are bound to change and change again. It seems that any number of people want me to be ashamed of who I am and what I have done. They'd rather see me fail so they can point and say, "You see? I told you she was no good!" They want me to feel like a leper, as though somehow I should be punished for what I've done.

It's all very reminiscent of a scene out of the film *Scarface,* when Al Pacino explodes in a crowded dining room, saying, "You're all assholes. You know why? 'Cause none of you got the guts to be what you want to be. You need people like me so you can point your fingers and say, 'Hey! There's the bad guy!'"

Don't get me wrong; it's not as if I would ever compare myself to a fictional gangster—I'll leave that to the rappers. What I am saying is that even in fiction we find truth, meaning, and relevance. This is a feeling so many of us have. I have heard the same emotions expressed by diverse parts of our society: from convicts looking for a new start to young, single mothers and high school dropouts. So many of us make bad decisions—poor choices that create a stigma—and we sometimes spend the rest of our lives trying to undo them. *Confessions of a Video Vixen* was a portrait of who I was: the good, the bad, and the ugly. I cannot write the same book again, because I am already evolving into a different person. I can only give you who I am now, and as I grow, so will my writing and my understanding of life.

Though *Confessions* was undoubtedly a memoir, I am now removed from that world and the woman it describes. I am no longer that young woman, wild and crazy, not thinking of her future or that of her child. In fact, my ex-boyfriend-turned-best-friend-and-confidant, Bill Maher, would often laugh and say how the rest of the world would be amazed to know how traditional I really am, how I am a fan of monogamy and relationships, how I cater to the man in my life, and how I take care of my household before anything else. Once, during the exhausting *Confessions* book tour, I canceled several important dates to join him on his tour. In fact, if I had it my way, I would work a lot less and spend more time with my son and with Bill, the man with whom I hope to spend the rest of my life.

Will I continue to defy other people's expectations? You better believe it. I have been willing to share my ideas with the world because what I know for sure is that when we discuss our ideas, our reasoning, and our mistakes with others, we improve our chances of touching someone else's life and evoking change in them. Even if someone disagrees with everything I say or do, at least they have realized that doing and saying everything exactly opposite from the way I do suits them best.

My goal as an author is to tell the truth as candidly as I can, so that those who have no one will at least have me. They can share my experiences and perhaps positively alter theirs. I have seen this effect firsthand; in fact, I have yet to host a lecture or a book signing and not see at least one young woman in my audience in tears. I have been receiving letters and e-mails over the past several years from young women who have been hurt in their lives and were unable to share their pain with anyone but me. I feel a sense of great responsibility to those women and women like them, who have been afraid and ashamed to call out for help. I want to help them to say they are wounded and in need of repair, to admit their wrongs and begin to make them right.

There are many wonderful things that have emerged from my new career, and there is much glamour in this Hollywood life. Yet it is not entirely true to say that it has all been worth it. There are days when I feel down and find it difficult to function in my new life because of a feeling of displacement. Throughout my life I have never been comfortable in groups, because I always feel like the "odd man out." There is something different about me: the way I think, the way I feel and express myself, my blunt honesty and awkward disregard for feelings hurt by the truth.

I have always felt, therefore, that I marched to the beat of a different drummer. This has both helped and hindered me over the years, but as I continue into adulthood it becomes more apparent that very few people in my life are like me. I often find myself shying away from those I have known for years. Our conversations have changed, our lives have become quite different, and I realize that in many ways I am an anomaly.

That realization doesn't always feel good. Some of my "old friends" are mothers, as I am, but they have no careers. Those friends who have careers, often have no children. Some of my acquaintances are unfocused, with no plan for their lives except maybe to get married and have children. Certainly, none of my oldest friends live their lives in a Hollywood bubble, in the public eye, as I do now. Our frames of reference are dramatically different, and I find myself learning more from my new friends, who live their lives publicly as well, making this bubble I live in seem even smaller.

I look around and find very few twenty-something successful writers with the responsibility of running publishing imprints while maintaining their own publishing careers, supporting small staffs, raising children, and carrying mortgages, to say nothing of doing so while seeing their faces plastered in the tabloids, on the Internet, and on television—and not always in a positive or truthful light.

As Bill would say, I'm sure there are people who wish they had my problems, and God knows I've had worse problems in the past. But this high life in Hollywood isn't always what it's cracked up to be, and that takes a little getting used to. I know that I have put myself in a position to be judged—the truth is that on some level we all do. My doing so publicly makes my experiences and emotions appear different, but I am quite human, too. That said, I wish this journey were less painful and that the whole world knew exactly what kind of person I really am. What I know for sure is that it's better to understand myself than to be understood. I understand so much more than I ever have, and part of that understanding is knowing that I cannot change the past but can most certainly continue to manifest a bigger and brighter future.

My father once said to me that the worst thing I ever did was to be born a girl, because if I were a man the things I've done would be either celebrated or overlooked. It seems as though only a man can make sleeping around, dealing drugs, going to jail, being under-educated, and being shot nine times cool and enviable or even worth mimicking.

I recognize the double standard, and in a perfect world I would prefer for men and women to be treated equally in all facets of life. But that may be just as impossible as establishing equal treatment between the races, between heterosexuals and homosexuals, or between the rich and the impoverished.

I will never fight for sexual equality, but I will always uphold my right to do and say whatever I wish, whenever I wish. I will ruffle feathers and make some people uncomfortable, but as long as I am always true to myself, I'll never lose sleep. In short, whether nay-sayers like it or not, I am evolving, changing for the better. "So say good night to the bad guy. You're never gonna see a bad guy like me again."

CHAPTER FIFTEEN

Beauty Is the Beast

An early morning conversation with Academy Award winner Jamie Foxx set forth a series of events and provoked a slew of emotions that have changed me. It's amazing how the typical evening can turn into anything, and how you can walk into a situation oozing with confidence, then walk out of it unsure of everything you've ever known.

It was five in morning in Los Angeles, and I was leaving my favorite speakeasy. That's what I like to call it, but the appropriate term for the establishment is "private membership community." The party starts at around one in the morning and carries on until five. The members of this special community are some of the most elite people in entertainment, friends of the elite, or, in some cases, friends of the friends. The party is held every Saturday night, but members of this private membership community never know where the party will be held until they receive an e-mail from the establishment announcing the location, which changes every weekend. In order to belong to this elite club of partygoers, one must pay a membership fee ranging anywhere from six hundred fifty to four thousand dollars a month. How much you pay depends on how many guests you want to bring, and whether it is an individual or corporate sponsorship.

In terms of star power, the admission is worth the tariff. On any given Saturday you could very well find yourself dancing shoulder to shoulder with the likes of Ryan Phillippe. At this particular gathering I spied Jamie Foxx, Janet Jackson, her boyfriend Jermaine Dupree, Kevin Federline, Lil Jon, and Ian Ziering of *Beverly Hills 90210* and now *Dancing with the Stars* fame.

The social structure within the club that night could easily be broken down into four hierarchical groups. First there were the celebrities, and they came in three different flavors: (A) famous, (B) trying to stay famous, or (C) becoming famous. The way they all moved around each other was reminiscent of honeybees in a hive. Then there were the wallflowers, who were like extras in a movie. They were there just to be surrounded by the famous. These were the happy smiling faces along sidelines—people who were content just to be there at all. There were a few sourpusses mixed in, though, and most of them were women. They were looking at me, my friends, and all the other celebrities with longing in their eyes and a hint of anger and jealousy behind them.

Kevin Federline arrived surrounded by friends and bodyguards. His expressions and body language spoke of a group C celebrity, someone in the process of becoming famous. These are the types who need to be seen; they come in with forty of their closest friends and rarely sit down once inside. They tend to work the room, walking around and making eye contact with almost everyone, not because they're noticing *you* but because they want you to notice *them*. Mostly they want to get close to the group A celebrities, as if their greater fame would rub off on them somehow or they would shine brighter in that reflected light.

I watched Kevin as he approached our group. He stood behind Jamie Foxx, waiting for the opportunity to shake hands with him.

Jamie, however, was heavy into a debate regarding the Dallas Cowboys and seemed to notice no one outside the group. Jamie was one of the few people in the club that night who were actually group A famous. Individuals in this category are more low-key and tend to stay within their groups for the most part. They most certainly do not go around trying to be noticed—these people get noticed enough without trying. In fact, most of the time they have the opposite problem—they get noticed too much.

After waiting a bit, K-Fed finally inched a bit closer and tapped Jamie on the shoulder. The interaction was extremely brief as Kevin offered his hand and said something like, "What's up, man?" Jamie partially turned toward Kevin, slapped his hand, grasped it, and brought him in for a split-second tap on the back.

"Yeah, what's up?" Jamie replied. Then he quickly turned his attention back to the Cowboys debate and those of us in the group. Not surprisingly, group A celebrities can be quite dismissive to fans and colleagues, because they are more in need of time and space. This described Jamie to a tee that night.

Jamie noticed something interesting about Janet Jackson and Jermaine Dupree that evening, and based on what he said, I took a closer look and tried to figure out what category those two fit into. It seems that here in the glory days of Beyoncé and Jay-Z, Janet Jackson and Jermaine Dupree have slipped a notch. They've become group B celebrities, trying to hang on and stay famous as a couple. There was a time when they were on top of the heap. Group B celebs would wait politely for a chance to say hello to Janet the way K-Fed waited for Jamie. No more. One thing about life in the public eye is that once you've gotten to the top, time is no longer on your side. One day you'll wake up and it'll be twenty years later. While you're riding high, somewhere in the world someone is being born who will take your place. Eventually even Beyoncé will have to step aside for a kid who's still in diapers today.

All this makes me think of my life and career, about the relationships I have now and the ones I wish to maintain. What I know for sure is that putting it all in perspective and keeping it there is going to be my ultimate test. I thought about which category I find myself in now and which I would like to be in when it's all said and done. Being famous can be just as great as it can be heartbreaking. I find myself more reclusive and trying to safeguard as much of my private life as possible, generally without success. And though I am extremely proud of my career and my decision to open my former life and ways to the world, at times it is a burden.

My life story becomes longer each time I am asked to tell it. I hate to hear myself discussing the answers to the simplest questions. These days when I am asked, "How did you get to Hollywood?" I answer obliquely, "That's a long story," and try to avoid going into any further detail. If people persist, sometimes, I just give the real answer and watch what happens.

"What made you move to L.A.?"

"My son's father used to beat me. I had to grab my infant son and run in the middle of the night. Los Angeles was the closest place where I had a friend. And you?" That usually shuts them up for a while.

Sometimes I wish for anonymity. I wish no one could see me, that they did not know my name. These are feelings I never thought I would have when I was dreaming this dream life as a child. I thought that once I did all this, it would be different for me—that I would be completely different and would automatically be happy. Not happening.

I sometimes feel guilty for being successful. I am uncomfortable with it at times and downplay it to friends. I find myself purposely trying not to get excited when something great happens in my life and career—when I spend another week on the *New York Times* best-seller list or acquire another book or television deal. I would like to think that this is caused solely by humility, but no—part of it is the feeling of unworthiness I have always felt, even when I have earned the accolades.

Inside there is always turmoil and doubt, but it's the outward appearances that make people tend to believe that all is well. It's the appearance of living well that makes others envy the lifestyle. As a woman it is commonplace to hear "But you're so pretty," when confiding in friends or perfect strangers about hardships in your life.

Beauty is like armor—a pretty face gives the impression that no harm has come to this heart, and the smile it projects implies happiness when, in fact, it only shelters heartache. I admitted many of these feelings in *Confessions*. That book served an undeniably necessary purpose in my life and the lives of those who have been touched by it. I have no regrets about the decision to open my life to the world, giving better insight into a culture rarely understood by outsiders. However, the fact is, I have changed since the stories in *Confessions* were a reality in my life, and I have changed even more since I published those sordid accounts. Although I wouldn't write that book today, I can say that because I have written it, my life has changed for the better.

It wasn't long before Jamie and I locked eyes during his Cowboys debate, and as he proclaimed why the team was the best in the league, I noticed that every few sentences he would reach out, touch my shoulder, and speak directly to me. I'm not a big football fan, but I listened intently and pretended I understood what he was talking about. I found him extremely captivating, and his touch made me want to know more about him. It was obvious he wanted to know more about me as well.

After his heartfelt Cowboys rant, Jamie turned to me and said, "Damn, you're pretty!" Then he turned to my friend Benny, who was standing right beside me, and said, "I don't know how you do it, man!"

I was ready to chime in with "Oh, no, we're just friends! I've known him for years," but Benny spoke right up and came to my rescue. "Me and Karrine?! No, I know her too well to date this broad. But she's the truth, though. Karrine is one of the realest people I know. She's a good girl."

Benny and I were not dating—that was the information Jamie was looking for when he asked the question. As Benny spoke, I could see Jamie's interest being sparked. He moved a few steps closer and behind me. We started swaying to the music, and Jamie placed his hands on my back and shoulders, gently yet effectively massaging them. He whispered in my ear, "You're tense; you should let me work these kinks out for you."

When Jamie Foxx offers to massage your body at four in the morning, after a bottle of champagne and two shots of Patrón, it's hard to say no. In hindsight it may seem naive on my part, but at that point it did not occur to me that the encounter would go any further than a massage. There was something about Jamie that led me to believe that I could trust him to do only what he said he would. He has that sort of character, or at least around me he did.

At the end of the evening, as the sun began to rise over Los Angeles, I found myself at Jamie's home along with several other friends. Over the next four hours, from five until shortly after nine in the morning, the two of us shared candid conversations about everything from the mundane to the marvelous. Sandwiched in between the two, there was also discussion about "Karrine Steffans"—well, not me exactly, but Karrine Steffans the video vixen.

From the way he spoke about her, I could tell Jamie had no idea that she and I were one and the same. For the entire time we interacted that morning, he had no idea that the Karrine whose back he had so happily massaged was *that* Karrine. I was just a girl to him, just a face, and he never once asked what I did for a living or who I really was. Even though he didn't ask, I did what I've come to do with all new people in my life: I supplied the clues so he could figure it out. As he began to put the pieces together, his eyes became big with surprise, and his mouth dropped open. "That's you?" he said as he jumped from the sofa. "You're *that* Karrine?"

It has been long said that pretty gets you in the door, but once you're in you'd better have something smart to say to keep you in the room. This is an adage that has proved true time and time again. Pretty, on its own, will never get you much of anything; its rewards are usually short-lived and shallow. It may get you the man of your desires, but it may keep him from ever getting to know the person behind the face. It may get you into the business, but which side of it, and at what cost? Pretty is as much a curse as a gift, especially if the woman has nothing of importance or intelligence to offer. A woman's body, looks, and mannerisms can be sexy, but there is nothing sexier or more enduring than a woman who can spark physical and intellectual interest and desire. Although looks rarely stand on their own merit, intelligence most always does.

I knew that the revelation that I was *that* Karrine would be a pivotal moment in our morning and would change the nature of my relationship with Jamie, but in what way, I could not be sure. He paced the room for a few minutes, then scratched his back against the wall and armoire, like a bear. "You know, after everything I've heard about you, I would have thought you were a real fucked-up individual," he said. "But you're not! You're cool as hell! I just had no idea that you were that girl!"

"*That girl.*" It seems as if, for the rest of my life, I'll be *that girl,* and I'm not sure how I feel about that. But in the wee hours that morning, it became clear to me that being *that girl* in this room was making Jamie increasingly uncomfortable. Earlier in the evening he was so free with his admissions and his feelings. He sat close to me and every so often would touch my shoulder or massage my neck. Now he stood clear across the room, staring at me as if I were the world's eighth wonder. Was he afraid of me because he didn't want to be part of the next book? Even after he slowly made his way back to the sofa, he sat several inches away, still staring. "You're a star," he said eventually. "I mean, you're not just a girl anymore. People know you; you're famous!"

"No, *you're* famous!" I responded. "You're the one with the Academy Award. I'm just a writer trying to make a living."

"You're a lot more than that, sweetie. You're *Karrine Steffans.*" So, yeah, he didn't want to end up in print.

All of a sudden, the intimate conversations stopped and the rest of the morning became about me. I felt like an alien. Being *that Karrine* set me apart from everyone else in the room. All the questions of the why and how of *Confessions* made my head spin, and I began to retreat into my shell. I became very quiet and withdrawn. This was one of those moments in life when I wished for invisibility, maybe a magic cloak like Harry Potter's. When he thought I was a just a girl, Jamie he was comfortable and unreserved with me, but once I became *Karrine Steffans,* author of *Confessions of a Video Vixen,* I became some sort of pariah.

All night we had let the good times roll, and now they came to a complete halt. I wanted to go home, and not just to my house, but home—the place where I'll belong for the rest of my life, the place where I'll be normal. In that instant I didn't want to be me and wished I *were* just a girl.

Though he was gracious and kind the entire time, I still felt like some interesting specimen in a petri dish, something to be marveled at, poked, and prodded. My thoughts drifted back to a conversation I'd had with Mike Tyson not long before this incident. Mike described the conditions of his new job in Las Vegas. He was being paid to train in an enclosed Plexiglas arena with patrons watching, cheering him on. He said he felt like an animal, like something under a microscope. As of this morning, I knew just how he felt.

Mike quit that gig shortly after our conversation, and sometimes I want to quit, too. For the next two or three days I cried. Between my evening and early morning with Jamie, the turmoil with Bobby, and going back and forth with Ray J in the previous weeks, I had emotionally crashed and burned. I was a virtual wreck at the bottom of a deep, blue, melancholy sea, drowning in who I was, wanting to be rescued by who I will be.

The beautiful people in Hollywood hide ugly secrets. I am no different from them in that regard. From those who *are* famous to those *trying to be* famous, to those *trying to remain* famous, we are all keeping up appearances. We are all smiling and carrying on as if we were not all scared to death of who we are and who we will be, and even more terrified that people will forget who we once were. Years down the road, no one wants to be asked that dreaded question, "Didn't you used to be somebody?"

It is our job to be beautiful—and simultaneously it is our curse. I find myself searching for love and piece of mind, for home and relevance. I hope for the day when my pretty face is eclipsed by my accomplishments, and when my "accomplishments" don't scare the shit out of Oscar winners. I hope for the day when the name Karrine Steffans stands alone, and *Confessions of a Video Vixen* is just the last entry on a long list of more important deeds. However, as optimistic as I am, even this seems an arduous and punishing task. Wish me luck.

Over the next several days, I lay in bed, depressed. Jamie had no idea that he made me cry all the way home and in the days that followed, but he made me feel as if I could never be normal and that I will always scare people. It was shortly after nine in the morning when I slid into my car and drove away from Jamie's home. It wasn't until I was getting into my car that Jamie admitted that though he had had every intention of giving me the massage my body so desperately needed, it was all just a setup to have sex with me. But that was when I was just a pretty girl to him. Once I turned into *that Karrine,* it was another story. In this instance, I guess being me is good when it makes people not want to have sex with me. I told Jamie before I left that I would write this chapter, and he gave me the perfect title for it: "Beauty Is the Beast." Thanks, Jamie, for the title— but most of all, for the lesson.

CHAPTER SIXTEEN

Enough Is Enough

Octber 18, 2006 was a good day at the tail end of several not-so-good ones. I was awakened that morning by the early sunrise and the sound of chirping birds outside my bedroom's French doors. I was slow to rise, dreading the hour-long drive ahead of me, because I was scheduled to appear in Children's Court. It had been nine months since my nervous breakdown and subsequent recovery. During those nine months, the court ordered me to see a psychologist and attend parenting classes. My son was also ordered to attend counseling sessions, and a social worker visited our home twice a month, every month.

This was the day that my case would be dismissed. After almost a year of going back and forth to court, I was anxious to have the ordeal come to an end. This was also the first morning I had to myself in a while. Bobby had been out of town for a little over a week, and though he was back in town, I wasn't exactly ready for him to visit my home again. With no one in the house except Naiim and me, I felt alive again.

The past few days had been a virtual roller coaster ride. I had to make decisions about my personal and business life that could very well change the direction of my immediate future. With Bobby Brown gone, I had to decide whether I wanted him around me ever again. There are so many things about him that are just plain wrong. He can be so disrespectful and hurtful at times, and I was very tired of fighting and crying with him, all in the name of saving his life. At the same time, he is one of the few people in the world who understand and accept me without judgment. On one hand, I knew I deserved better company, because I have had better. On the other hand, I wondered what could be better than someone who knows you completely—your secret thoughts and desires. With all my quirks and all his shortcomings, we work. But because of those very same quirks and shortcomings, we don't. We are often the best of friends and the worst of enemies.

The air in Los Angeles was cooling, and as autumn made its way into the city, I found it more difficult to sleep in my cold and quiet home. I missed his antics and jokes, and the sound of his voice trying desperately to hold the high notes he once sang with ease. I wondered if maybe the companionship was the only reason for my longing and if I would still want him around when the warm, busy summer drew near. Bobby has been a weakness of mine since the day we met. He was also so engaging, and like many of his friends, I find it hard to turn my back on him, knowing his potential for both kindness and failure. But before Bobby, there was Ray J.

Ray and I started seeing each other again early in the summer 2006, and by the end of it, all the magic we made six years before was erased and seemed as if it had never happened. The first time around, he was eighteen and I was twenty-one. Now, at twenty-five and twenty-eight, we were two different people trying to recapture a lost love that had since been superseded by many others. As I lay in bed, lonely, I scrolled through my phone book looking for a familiar name—someone who would make me feel safe, even if only for one night. To me, there could be no one safer than Ray J, and I had no hesitation in giving him a call. He and I had recently bumped into each other at a local nightclub, and from the moment I saw him, those old feelings came rushing back. We were something back then; what we could be now was yet to be seen.

During a brief conversation, we made plans to meet later that evening—or rather, early the next morning. It was four a.m. when we pulled into Mel's Diner on Sunset Boulevard for an early morning breakfast with friends. We sat shoulder to shoulder in a booth and nestled over two mugs of hot tea. I wrapped my right arm around his left and entangled myself in my past. I smelled his cologne and rubbed the back of his neck, imagining what it would be like to be with him once more. It had been years for us, and I pictured fireworks once I got him alone. I wouldn't have to wonder too much longer. Two hours later, we checked into a suite at L'Ermitage Hotel in Beverly Hills.

So, there we were—old friends, old lovers, with no idea what to do. The conversation was downright pathetic as we talked about our broken relationships, his with Kim Kardashian and mine with Bill. We were two wounded animals trying to find pleasure in someone from our past in order not to deal with the devastation of our present. He sat in a chair and I perched on the corner of the bed as we caught up on how our lives had been since the last time we spoke. We both wanted to be with someone else, but all we had that night was each other. Well, it would have to do for the moment.

Like mannequins, we clumsily found our way to the bed and shed our clothes. Stiff and uncomfortable, we forced the issue and had the most painful sex anyone could ever have—my round with Mike Tyson excepted. In situations like this, there is nothing worse than being with someone out of convenience when your heart would rather be with the one you love. Ray J was no longer the young man I'd known before; now he was just as broken as I was, and as he climbed on top and mechanically maneuvered, I looked at him and knew he wasn't really with me. I wasn't really with him, either. I closed my eyes and silently mouthed, "Bill . . . Bill." It was six in the morning before the ordeal was over, and as soon as I knew he was asleep I slid out of bed, dressed, and escaped. Ray is one of those people I will always love, and whenever I see him I am drawn to what he has always meant to me since we first met in 2000. But the image I once had of us together was gone.

Still, we gave it another shot just a week later, with the same results. Back at L'Ermitage, I listened to him tell me he loved me still. He talked as if there were a future to be had. We reminisced about how good we used to be, and laughed at some of our funniest memories. He pulled a bottle of Veuve Clicquot Rosé champagne out of his overnight bag and poured us each a glass. He turned on the radio, grabbed me around my waist, and slow-danced with me to the music as he sang along. He was saying everything I wanted to hear; it was the same speech he gave me a week earlier, and there I was, wanting to believe it again. This night felt different from the time we spent a week before. I was hoping against hope that maybe, just maybe, my old friend was back.

As we headed toward the mattress again, it felt more organic and more like home, just the way I needed it to feel. We both knew that in our hearts we wanted to be somewhere else, with someone else, but in that moment we made do and made a memory. He was soft and sensuous, slow and romantic. His lips cushioned mine, and with my eyes closed I could have sworn he was eighteen again and that I would be all right. I wanted so badly to be impressed by someone and to counteract the effects of being with Bobby—someone who makes sure you can never be impressed by him.

The irony of it all was that I had wanted Bobby in my life originally to shake things up after my breakup with Bill. I wanted wild fun and uncontrollable fits of laughter again. With Bill, it was all so safe and planned out: the seven o'clock bath, the nine o'clock dinner, reading the paper and working in the office until three in the morning, sleeping until one in the afternoon. At first I craved the stability of the regimen, but it became mundane, and all of a sudden I wanted chaos. That's my sickness, and coupled with Bobby's sickness, I got a whole lot more than I bargained for. Between Bobby's habit of driving my car with an open container of beer—even with my son in the backseat—and his insatiable need to get high and stay awake for days, then sleep for days, I was exhausted.

I secretly wanted to be swept off my feet and be shown the things I'd seen once before: parties and shots of tequila set ablaze at the hottest nightclub in Los Angeles, Miami, Las Vegas, or New York. I longed to have someone young and alive in my life again, a man with his whole life ahead of him, with no fear and no rules and, if at all possible, very little baggage. That was Ray, way back then, and it mostly describes him today, except for one thing. A lot can happen—and has—in the six years since he and I had been together. The young man I fell in love with then was now all grown up and carrying baggage. After our second encounter, I slipped quietly out of the suite as I had the first time, in order to see my son off to summer camp by eight in the morning. As I was leaving the hotel I began to doubt that Ray and I were doing the right thing. To put it plainly, we were using each other, trying to fill a void, and our relationship could never be meaningful again under these circumstances. He was broken by his recent breakup with Kim, and I was still crying myself to sleep over Bill and had no business being there with him.

I must be a glutton for punishment, because these feelings didn't stop me from seeing him yet again, this time at his condominium near my home. He had recently moved in and hadn't yet furnished the place, except for a few showpieces left over from when the condo was being shown as a model. On the first floor of the three-story building was a daybed, cluttered with junk.

We were like animals as we tore away at the sheets, throwing them to the floor. We ravaged each other's clothing and naked bodies as we pounded and sweated in unison. This was the height of our brokenness. We made love as if we hated each other—and, in fact, we did. We hated each other because neither of us was what the other wanted, but it was the best we could do at the time. I hadn't seen him this sexually engaged since six years ago. He was a beast, rough and sporadic. And still, the ever-hopeful lover inside me wondered, what if? What if we connected right here, right now, and managed to forget about everyone else, the way we had before? I was insane.

We carried on with energetic sex for an hour or more, pushing and pulling, screaming and moaning, kissing and biting, but when it was over, it was really over. All that was left were those two awkward mannequins from before. As I lay in the afterglow, Ray jumped to his feet and began to get dressed. It was as if none of it had ever happened, so I did the same and prepared to go back to my life without Ray—a few shreds of dignity short.

I put on a brave front as we walked out the door and slid into our cars, but on the way home I cried. I wasn't sure why at the time; in retrospect, I know that I cried because I had to move forward. I knew that going back to people I once loved may have seemed safe, but it was, in fact, more dangerous than moving ahead. I was running the risk of being disappointed by people for whom I had so much hope and expectation—all for the sake of fear. I was afraid of what my life would be if I weren't holding on to at least one thing, one person from my past. Who am I without who I *was*? I would find myself fighting with this question for the remainder of 2006.

Later that evening I changed my telephone number and vowed never to speak to him again. It was all too much to bear, questioning my decisions and myself. After leaving Ray, I spent the next few days in a funk. Should I give up on Bobby? Should I talk to Ray again, ever? I lay in bed for days, my head spinning with "should I's," and then the decisions were made. Enough is enough.

With that out of the way, there was one more issue at hand: Bobby. Like Lemony Snicket, my relationship with him had gone through a series of unfortunate events, and just as Lemony announced the end of the series, so did I. I threw his clothes into garbage bags and put them outside the front door. I called him and let him know he was no longer allowed in my home, my life, and, most crucially, the life of my son. And though I was secure in this decision, it hurt me to my core. I had given him all I could, more than anyone could have offered him; then he disgraced the time we shared, and disgraced me.

I lay on the couch for one full day, crying, shaken, and depressed. I shut off most of the world, and the few people I spoke to seemed only to aggravate the situation with their I-told-you-so's. I was sick and tired of it all and needed a voice of reason to pull me out of this funk. Here's the truth: no amount of money, fame or possessions will ever take the place of love and happiness. None of my personal issues have gone away or faded with the advancement of my career. Those issues only decrease with time, life experience, and introspection. I have a long way to go.

For moral support and an instant pick-me-up, I called Bill. There are very few men in the world who are equipped to be a Daddy. The man who can carry this title is smart enough in all subjects: politics, finances, life, and love. He is caring and compassionate and is always there to support and uplift the people he loves, and never leaves them. This is who Bill is and what he does for me. On this particular night, the last night of my pain, Bill gave me simple but perfect advice in an unusual and politically incorrect package.

Bill told me, in his infinite wisdom, that Joseph Stalin (no one's favorite person) had a saying he used to justify the grotesque killings he ordered and carried out: "No person—no problem." Though the words come from a historic villain, the concept is easy to understand. Whoever in my life is hurting me has to be let go, no matter how painful it may be. If there is no person, there most certainly will be no problem. These simple words from my Daddy meant the world to me, and I knew that waking up tomorrow would be easier than today. Enough is enough.

Before going to bed, however, I called Ray J. He and I hadn't spoken since our last encounter in the condo, but based on the sort of week and night I was having, I knew it was time either to cut my losses or to retain friendships, and none of that could happen without my being honest with myself and the people involved. We spoke for nearly an hour, and between the laughter and miscellaneous ranting, we managed to smooth over our personal issues. There would be no way for us to continue to carry on the way we had. I was looking for a place to belong and really needed to be alone, instead of trying to find someone to fill the space that my breakup with Bill had left in my life. I tried to fill that void by occupying my time and home with Bobby, and as soon as he was gone I recruited Ray to take his place. Just as I was about to reveal this to Ray, he told me he had recently begun an affair with Bobby's wife, Whitney Houston. My mouth fell open with amazement—and, I confess, no small amount of joy. It was at that moment our situation became even more sick and twisted.

Just a few weeks earlier, while Bobby and I were having lunch at a nearby Chinese restaurant, he was served with divorce papers. Though everyone around him saw it coming, Bobby lived in his own world, where everything was all right, where he didn't have a drug and alcohol problem, and where, no matter how much his wife insisted he stay away, their marriage was perfect. That was the day that our friendship went from unhealthy to potentially dangerous. Bobby spun even more out of control, lashing out at those closest to him and all who tried to help him, often declaring, "I don't need no help!"

I suspected why Ray J told me about himself and Whitney: he wanted me to help spread the word, especially to my friends in the press. Ray was looking for attention; he craved having his name in the tabloids, and as an attention whore, he was willing to do anything to achieve this. But as he continued to talk, I felt a developing personal satisfaction in having this information.

Ray may have been looking for press, but I was out for revenge. After all the things Bobby had done and said to hurt me, after insisting that I had done nothing for him while he was sleeping in my home, eating my food, driving my car, and spending my money, I now saw a way to hurt him back. Bobby's Achilles' heel has always been his wife and his children. Even though he had been served with divorce papers, he still insisted that he and Whitney would soon reconcile. Those around him knew differently. So after Ray and I concluded our conversation, ending it on good terms, with an understanding just to be friends, my next call was to Bobby.

"Hello?" he answered.

"Hey, B, it's Karrine."

I could hardly wait to get the news out, to tear his heart apart and hurt him the way he'd hurt me. I wanted him to go to bed that night with the image of his wife with another man, a man he knew, a man younger, more handsome, and more successful than he, a man he could run into anywhere and at any time on the streets of Los Angeles.

"What are you calling *me* for? I thought you hated my guts!"

"No, never that. But you know what's fucked up?"

"What, babe . . . ?"

"How Ray J is fucking your wife right now."

"What! Man, where'd you hear that?"

"Straight from the horse's mouth."

"No way."

"Yep, and I heard she loved it . . . and she should—he *is* so fucking good at it!"

There was silence on the other end of the line.

"But listen, B, I have to go. Have a good night."

And with that, I was done and able to go bed, satisfied.

Ray and I came to an understanding that night, and I came to the conclusion that Bobby and I never will, and that Bill and I will always understand each other. I also learned that it's okay to cry again and to love unconditionally, even and especially if you never get it back—because God will always repay those who give self- lessly. My blessings are on the way. I learned when to say "enough is enough," and how to know when it's not.

CHAPTER SEVENTEEN

Love after Death

On November 10, 2006, the world awoke to the somber news that R & B legend Gerald Levert had passed away. He died from an apparent heart attack, caused by an inadvertent combination of over-the-counter and prescription drugs. I had known Gerald over the past four years and had starred in one of his videos for the single *Funny.* I was stunned to hear of his passing at just forty years old, but several people close to me who knew him better than I did were even more devastated, especially New Edition member Johnny Gill.

Johnny called me as soon as he heard the news. I cringed while listening to him on the other end of my telephone that morning as he cried out for the man he called his brother. Cringing may not have been the compassionate response, but then, I don't do death well. I have never been good at dealing with it, and in the past I have found it difficult to support those who are touched by its sobering grip. Nevertheless, I tried my best to be there for my friend as he depended on me for support, and helping him grieve led me to take a look at myself as well.

Over the next few days, Gerald's passing lent itself to my

contemplation of death, both literal and figurative. Unable to mourn Gerald's death, I was forced to confront my willingness to mourn those who are still living but have simply left my life. Bobby and I had been apart for a little more than a month. There were nights when I missed him to the point of tears; there are still some of those nights. As time goes on, those moments happen less and less often; still, they exist.

There are also moments now and then when I stop and think of Ray J. We are now just friends, but I miss the way we used to be, and feel sorry for the fact that we can never be that way again. After a few times of trying to reconnect, it became painfully obvious to me that there is no way we could ever be as close as we once were.

Then there is Papa, the now infamous secret lover I spoke of in *Confessions*, with whom I carried on a five-year affair despite the fact that he was married for the last four. I eventually left Papa to begin a life with Bill. I miss Papa for so many different reasons and sometimes question whether letting him go was the right thing. There are nights when I wonder where he is and whether he thinks of me still. I miss all the days we spent talking about our lives, together and apart. We talked a lot about my future, and he assured me I would be successful one day.

It was hard for me to walk away from him, but I did so knowing that I could not be with Bill the way I wanted to and still have a relationship with Papa at the same time. I made this decision just two days after meeting Bill, knowing somehow that he would be the love of my life. In retrospect, I'm glad I ended my love affair with Papa, but I wish I could have preserved our friendship.

Whether as friends or as lovers, I miss having all these men in my life. In my own way, I mourn the fact that these relationships are dead, never to be resurrected, and that is a truth that was difficult for me to face. But life has a way of giving you no choice, and for that I am grateful.

As I tried my best to help Johnny through one of the toughest times of his life, I was reminded of my grandfather's passing twenty years earlier. I was given the news of his death while in school one day—they called me to the office and handed me the telephone. When my mother told me he was dead, I was overcome with sadness. It was like watching a home movie—instantly, frames of the days spent with my grandfather flashed through my mind. I knew there would be no more days in Brooklyn, watching reruns of *All in the Family* while eating Spam sandwiches. I knew I'd never hold his hand again as we walked to his office. I wondered who would sit at his desk now that he was gone.

Nevertheless, I was unable to shed a tear, for fear of being seen. Even at seven years old, I wanted to be strong and keep up a brave front. I thought that crying would make me look weak. In the days that followed, I remember family members scurrying about, preparing for his funeral service. Every so often bouts of crying would break out. I cried too, but I didn't let anyone see me. I locked myself in the bathroom, ran the faucet in the sink, and cried for my grandfather. I cried into a towel to muffle the sound; I cried so hard, my face hurt. I cried until there were no tears left.

The day of the funeral I still didn't want anyone to see me cry. I thought my grandfather would be proud of me if I could hold it together and be brave in front of everyone. As the rest of the family and friends who attended the service cried, throwing handfuls of soil and sprinkling holy water atop the casket, I stiffened my upper lip and straightened my spine. I bit the inside of my cheeks and held my breath, off and on, while reciting to myself, *Do not cry . . . do not cry.*

And I didn't. When the funeral was over, we all headed out of the cemetery and toward the exit. I was glad that the ordeal was over—my head ached from the pressure of holding back my tears. I was just breathing a sigh of relief that the worst was over, when my mother started in on me. She pulled me to the side and scolded me for not crying.

I stood there in horror as she ripped into me verbally. Every inch of me wanted to scream, "I cried already! I cried for thirty minutes in the bathroom!" but all I could do was stand there as she clutched my scrawny arms. Truth be told, I wanted to cry right then and there, but I held back out of sheer stubbornness. I didn't want her or the rest of the family and friends to think she was getting the best of me. If I hadn't cried at the sight of my dead grandfather lying in his casket, I most certainly would not give *her* his tears. I thought I was doing the right thing by holding it all in. I thought my grandfather would be proud.

That was over twenty years ago, and I have since come to understand that crying is not a sign of weakness but actually proof of normality. Still, when it comes to death I have a hard time either understanding or giving in to the mourning process. I can't grieve for the dead, but as soon as a relationship ends, I have no problem falling onto the floor and lamenting that my life is over. What the fuck is that about? Does love mean more to me than life itself? Do I cherish lovers more than I do the lives of friends?

As I listened to Johnny sob and sniffle over the phone, I began to grieve for him, even though he was very much still here. I began to think, *What if this is the last time I'll hear his voice? What if he never wakes up tomorrow?*

Johnny and I first saw each other at the home of Eddie Murphy during an Easter celebration. We never spoke that day and didn't see each other again until that night at the Greek Theatre in Los Angeles when Bobby and I resumed our friendship. Johnny and I exchanged numbers that night. After that, we spoke on the telephone almost every day.

It got to the point where I began to think he was something of a pest. Johnny became like an annoying older brother who always thought he had the answers to all the big questions in my life. He offered long, boring speeches to prove his point. At first I didn't think I liked him all that much. He was nice enough, but not necessarily my type of friend. Still, we kept in touch, and over time he began to grow on me. Even while I was with Bobby, Johnny and I would spend platonic nights together or talk for hours on hours on the telephone.

It took Gerald's passing for me to fully appreciate him and for our friendship to deepen. Johnny had been there for me every night I cried, every time Bobby didn't come home or did something inappropriate. He listened to my heartache, and now I was listening to his. With each phone call, he became more of a real person to me, vulnerable and afraid. I began to feel things for him that I never imagined I would, and those feelings felt a lot like love. Not love in a romantic sense, but more a love and respect for the caring person I now saw him to be—a person very different from the long-winded, finger-pointing older brother I had pegged him for earlier in our relationship.

Of course, he wasn't the one who changed; I was. He was there this entire time, and I did little more than ignore him. I'm not sure if this discovery foreshadowed a romantic relationship in the future, but for now I am sure that Johnny is the kind of person I am ready for: a kinder, gentler man who is there when I need him and knows he can rely on me for support under the most difficult circumstances. Nevertheless, my love for Bill makes it difficult to truly let anyone else in.

In the meantime, it's good to have a friend like Johnny, and I am positive he would agree that it was a delight to have a friend like Gerald, who helped me to realize that even though death may be difficult for me to deal with, it is the one thing that is proof positive of just how special life is and how important it is to treat the special people in it well. I no longer want to let the good guys pass me by, nor do I want any man to hold the weight of my world on his shoulders. Death is final; breakups are not, and I know that in the future I would rather cry for the finality of death rather than for the fleeting discomfort of a love lost. And I have Gerald and Johnny to thank for teaching me that.

CHAPTER EIGHTEEN

Disclaimer

The Monday before Thanksgiving 2006, I found myself at the Hollywood hotspot Hyde. The establishment is located, as most trendy nightclubs are, on the notorious Sunset Strip, but unlike at most watering holes on Sunset, it is nearly impossible to gain entry into Hyde unless you are an undeniable A-list celebrity or know someone on the inside. The latter is the reason I was there that night, as I am most Monday nights, enjoying a glass of a woodsy cabernet sauvignon and the company of my nameless boy toy. On any given night at Hyde, you'll find yourself hobnobbing with the likes of Paris Hilton and Lindsay Lohan.

On this night, however, I found myself sitting shoulder to shoulder with international heartthrob Colin Farrell and, later in the evening, looking upward as I jotted down the number of a towering Keenan Ivory Wayans. It was a typical Monday night in Tinsel Town as the paparazzi lined the sidewalk, most of them working under contract to Hollywood news-and-gossip lord TMZ.com. Amid bulbs flashing and names being called out, I made my way through the mob and into my car, boy toy in tow. The results of my shoulder rubbing with Colin will have to wait until another time and place—it is a conversation I had with Keenan the next day that shapes this chapter.

At about three the following afternoon, Keenan and I engaged in an hour-long phone chat that left me with a wonderful impression of the man. Our conversation began as most informal introductions do, with light conversation about the impending holidays and the harmless questions about family and friends. Then, about forty-five minutes into the conversation came the inquiry I always dread: "So, what do you do?"

Ah, the oh-so-necessary disclaimer—the "I'm the girl who wrote that book" speech. Since my morning under the microscope with Jamie Foxx, it was a speech I dreaded giving more than ever. There was a lump in my throat as I recited my rehearsed speech, beginning with "I am an author. I write internationally best-selling nonfiction."

"Really? That's great!" said Keenan. "What are your books about?"

"Well, my first was memoir, and my second is . . . well, it's also a memoir. I'm not so sure what the third will be."

After I explained more about my career and the initial reaction of the general population to *Confessions*, he said, "I know your book. I read it." I swallowed and waited for the onslaught but instead received a compliment. "I didn't find it to be as jaw-dropping as everyone made it out to be. As a matter of fact, I know there had to be more to many of the stories, and that you held back. I like that. After working in this town for so long, I've seen them come and go. *Confessions* is the story of many women in Hollywood, and I've even known some worse stories than I read in your book."

I was relieved, to say the very least. Unlike in my previous conversation with Jamie, Keenan seemed to open up even more on realizing who I am. He was smart and witty, and I reveled in the musings of an older, wiser man. Being just a few years younger than Bill, Keenan bantered in a way reminiscent of the love of my life. I was reminded just then of how much I appreciate the time and attention of someone who has a lot to teach me. As he talked, I listened and learned.

But I know it won't always be like this. Many times it will be just as it was with Jamie. I know that when I travel in certain circles, I'll have to wear *Confessions* on my sleeve. Strangely enough, this seems to be necessary only in black Hollywood, which, thankfully, is a very small part of my life—and of Hollywood itself. I would hate to have to justify my existence to everyone I meet. I am not sure if Keenan and I will ever speak again or, if so, what the friendship will entail, but I do know that it's nice to be listened to and not judged unfairly. It's a pleasure to share ideas with those who want to know more about Karrine Steffans the individual rather than Karrine Steffans the vixen. And as I grow and continue to strive for more intellectual stimulation, it's refreshing to come across those who can supply it— who, unfortunately, are also a very small percentage of the populace in this town.

As we neared the Thanksgiving holiday, reports surfaced that Chris Rock filed for divorce from his wife of nearly ten years. That news prompted me to recall a few of the highlights of my friendship with Chris, and brought back memories of a vicious rumor that he and I once had an affair. After meeting Chris in December 2000 at a Magic Johnson Christmas party, he and I became fast friends and confidants. He would share personal stories, anecdotes, and adventurous tales with me, one of which included a man I would later come to know as Anthony Pelicano.

Anthony Pelicano had become known in Hollywood as the man who could make any problem go away. A private detective, he reportedly was regularly hired to help in legal cases involving many A-list celebrities. He allegedly used unlawful methods to conduct his investigations, including wiretapping, illegal background checks, and enlisting law enforcement buddies to access state files.

It was a cold, rainy night in 2002 at the Beverly Hills Hotel when

Chris Rock talked to me about his paternity scandal from years before. Chris and I had been friends for some time, and we were having dinner with mutual friends and colleagues at the hotel's Polo Lounge. Chris had been hit with a paternity suit in 1999. At the time, a Hungarian model claimed to be carrying his child. Chris believed that it was all a setup, because the mother-to-be was pushed onto him by another man she was with on the night she and Chris first met.

I was told that after the investigation concluded, the Hungarian's child proved not to be Chris's. Chris then told me that the mother was later deported based on facts uncovered during the investigation. Was this the work of Pelicano behind the scenes? Did he use his friends in high and low places to affect the outcome of the investigation and hustle her out of the country? I don't know, but what I do know is that I have been told a lot of things by many powerful people, and it may not all make sense initially, but eventually it all comes together. When I saw news reports about Pelicano, featuring photographs of Chris Rock, I couldn't help but wonder if Pelicano was indeed the cleanup man.

Chris once told me that if I made a mistake, he would send the cleanup man after me. We laughed it off then, but I'm not laughing now. On hearing the news about his alleged involvement with Pelicano and putting the pieces together, it made me think.

There have been many times in my life when I have played with fire, and though I have been scorched and even ignited on several occasions, my burns have been minor in comparison to what could have been. For my own safety, happiness, and well-being, some things will always remain secret. I hate to make this town sound like a gangster-riddled crime novel, but the truth is, there are people here that you simply do not want to cross.

No, you may not end up sleeping with the fishes, but there are lots of other ways to die in this town. The most effective is the conspiracy of silence. You'll knock on the door of a producer, a Hollywood mover and shaker you've known for years, and all of a sudden that door no longer opens. That man no longer takes your calls. Green-lighted projects get canceled. Your agent drops you. Your manager does the same. Your career mysteriously stalls. This is the place where dreams are made, so naturally, this is also the place where they are often dashed. And while some people have criticized me for naming names, what I know is this: there are certain names you never mention, and there are names you give but only in the kindest light.

As Chris filed for divorce, the rumor surfaced that I was on the verge of including a chapter about him and our supposed past intimate relationship in this book. As usual, those published reports would prove incorrect. Initially, I had no intention of mentioning Chris at all or detailing any aspects of our past relationship. I choose to protect Chris for the sole reason that as long as I have known him, he has been nothing but a friend to me.

I am saddened by most reports of divorce, especially when there are children involved. Because I am a product and a participant of a broken home, I am all too familiar with the torture and irreversible damage one can wreak on children as well as on the adults involved.

For the record, Chris and I have spent time together in the past, though none of those moments have ever been romantic or sexual. They were, however, extremely intimate as we shared pieces of our lives in confidence. We would talk for hours on end about his work, my life, and his marriage. He always told me to be sure to use my "super powers" before I lose them. What he meant was that I should find a good man and settle down before my youthful sex appeal withers away. I'm not quite sure if that was such good counsel. I would hate to schedule my life around some clock or believe that I am only as good as my looks and sexual prowess.

Funny, but that little piece of advice says a lot about his feelings concerning love and marriage, not to mention the jabs he takes at both in his stand-up routines. As I see it, the world doesn't need me to explain my relationship and my conversations with Chris. What I would like the world to know is that in my time of need he was there, helping my son and me keep our heads above water, and for that I will be eternally grateful.

In the game of six degrees of separation, one has up to six links in a chain of friends and acquaintances connecting them to any other person. In my life, it seems I can make the connection in just one link most of the time. Because of that and the fact that most of my connections are men, many people automatically assume that those connections are sexual. Worse, many avid readers of the gossip columns are all too ready to believe that I'm a world class homewrecker, that I have had a hand in many of Hollywood's most public divorces, breakups, and scandals. In addition to the rumors about my relationships with Chris Rock and Bobby Brown, there have been mentions of my past dealings with Eddie Murphy. All these men have been linked to me in intimate ways, and I am delighted to report that it's all rubbish.

Eddie Murphy and I are virtual strangers, even though I have been to his home several times for Easter, boxing matches, and other social gatherings. He and Johnny Gill are the best of friends, more like brothers, and that's the closest I get to Eddie on a regular basis. The rumor started simply because I was at his home one night to view the last three rounds of a boxing match. That's all!

Interestingly enough, the rumors don't bother me at all. In my opinion, if some people spend the day sitting around and making up things about me, that is an honor. It only validates my existence and my ability to evoke emotion and interest in others. To me, that's pretty neat. But I live in a bubble, and those who know and love me do not. So, although rumors like these may not bother me, many times they bother those who are connected to me and who know

The Vixen
Diaries
128

they are not true. My friends often say, "I wish the world knew what kind of person you really are and that all of this is made up."

I feel as if those who follow my life and career may expect that there would be more to my relationships with powerful men in the entertainment industry. More often than not, I find nothing sexier than profound and intellectually lucrative friendships with the men in my life. One of the most important secrets of my success has been my acquaintance with some of the world's most powerful and influential men in film, television, music, fashion, literature, and even government, and most of those relationships are nonsexual. I snicker to think of how simple the public and media can be, missing the big picture and never thinking deep or far enough.

When I look back on my past and current relationships, I feel privileged to have been able to learn from some of the most successful businessmen in the nation, and to have the opportunity to learn from every one them on both small and larger scales. A lot of who I am as a woman is due to the men who have crossed my path, most especially Bill. I feel blessed to have the life I do and friends who have inspired and taught me. In my opinion, people ought not to be so concerned about who I'm sleeping with, but about who I am learning from.

CHAPTER NINETEEN

Any Given Monday

After getting rid of Bobby, Ray J, and a few other pieces of dead weight, I began to enjoy my time as a single woman on the town. This newfound life included a few new friends, one of whom I affectionately refer to as The Boy Toy. Every Monday night, while most people in this country are snuggled safely in their beds, sleeping and dreading the next day's workload and responsibility, I am out prowling the streets of Hollywood, with The Boy Toy close behind.

The evening begins in my bedroom as I decide what the ensemble for the evening will be and the mood it will reflect. Deciding on my mood for the evening is usually the most difficult part of the experience, since I am usually asleep by eight and struggle to get out of the bed, into the shower, dressed, and on the road. But this is my one night out, my only chance at an adult-friendly good time. So I jump out of bed and glide onto the relatively calm roadways. In Los Angeles the weekends are playtime for the majority, while the weekday nights are for the artists, socialites, riffraff, and trust fund babies. I like to think of myself as an artist—God knows I don't quite fit into any of the other categories. Still, the weekday nights are for those of us who don't have to awaken weekday mornings. Those nights are luxuries reserved for the people who can sleep late and keep the ringers of their telephones turned off well into midday.

There are only a couple of rules for my friendship with The Boy Toy, one of which is that we see each other only on Monday nights. After finally ridding myself of Bobby and having my new house all to myself for the first time since moving in, it feels good to be alone and single. It's a treat to be in control of my life and loves, and for the first time in a long time I am enjoying not wanting a relationship. Instead, I have a handsome, well-dressed companion in The Boy Toy.

I am growing increasing comfortable with my new life as a single, stress-free mom, and take great pride in my career and new home. Personally, I feel it's a great time in my life to be selfish and not share any more with another than I want to share. I have given myself and my time to men often enough, and each time it has been more headache than it's worth. For too many years I was someone else's girl toy. I've turned the tables. On Monday nights, like clockwork, I jump into my car and head for Hollywood to pick up The Boy Toy by ten.

The Boy Toy is a special pleasure of my new life. Not only can I enjoy the freedom of not having a boyfriend but, for the first time in over three years, I am sharing personal time with someone who is not connected to any of the entertainment industries, either behind the scenes or in front the camera. Though The Boy Toy is well connected on the club scene, he seems to know very little about my lifestyle outside our friendship. Though he knows exactly who I am since my life is literally an open book called *Confessions,* he is not concerned with my business, and that's nice for a change.

There is something very empowering about pulling up to a studio apartment in the heart of Hollywood in one of my brand-new Mercedes Benzes, honking my horn, and seeing The Boy Toy eagerly emerge. Sometimes I meet him near the club and he leaves his car around the corner. The Boy Toy jumps into mine, in an attempt to impress his friends. With a secret smile, I remember those days of clinging to the possessions of others in order to make myself feel worthy of the Hollywood scene. How happy I am to be free of that farce and finally to be comfortable in my own skin. For the first time, the man sitting next to me is not the breadwinner, and the luxury car he sits in is mine. There is nothing he can do for me except show me a good time. And that is all I ask of him.

Our first stop of the evening may be to grab a bite to eat at Katana or any cozy, dimly lit bistro in town. Or we may head straight to Hyde, one of the most exclusive clubs on the Sunset Strip. After a few drinks there, the night usually ends at Area, another Hollywood hotspot plagued by the paparazzi. Area is a much louder, larger, and busier venue than Hyde. I have yet to see the entire club, since The Boy Toy and I usually grab a seat among his friends and stay there.

Area is the kind of place where almost anything goes. On one particular night it was nothing less than a scene right out of the famous New York City club Studio 54, or so I would imagine. The tables were elegantly dressed with silver-plated buckets of ice and carafes of various liquors and juices. Glasses, napkins, and drinking straws lay strewn about the tabletops. You would notice nothing unusual about the table's inhabitants or accessories at first. On closer inspection, however, you would notice something very different about the clear plastic drinking straws that were being handed out around the table by the people we were sitting with. Each of the straws was packed with cocaine. They resembled a candy I enjoyed as a child, named Pixy Stix. These days, candy is still a crowd favorite, although now it's for the nose.

To avoid having to bend down and inhale lines of cocaine from the tabletop, which would have been conspicuous, the young men and women stuck the coke-filled drinking straws in their nostrils and breathed in the narcotic. Decked out in sunglasses and hooded sweatshirts, some were already dancing on the tables and couches in the dimly lit establishment. At one point I excused myself and went to the bathroom just to escape the scene for a moment. Comically, I was met by four women snorting lines off the sink, and two others having oral sex in the stall—Hollywood nightlife at its best. After washing my hands, I headed back to rejoin my Boy Toy just in time to see him, thankfully, refuse a helping of cocaine.

The excess and abuse was everywhere, but I did my best to ignore it as The Boy Toy and I turned to each other for conversation. The scene was incredible, and at any moment I expected Bianca Jagger to come through the center of the club on a white horse, as she had done at Studio 54 thirty years ago. It amazes me how many people are in such a rush to head to this madhouse, having no idea what they are really getting into; how many people believe what they see in movies and read in the tabloids. This place seemed so glossy and perfect before I moved here, but I was quickly reminded that fairy tales are only alive in children's books. So many people have fantasies of Hollywood, not knowing that Hollywood Boulevard itself is lined with homeless and drug-addicted teens, panhandling throughout the day and night, to say nothing of the transvestite prostitutes just a block away on Sunset, ten minutes east of the Strip.

True, wonderful things can and do happen here, just as in other parts of the world. But few places on earth can corrupt a soul quite the way Los Angeles can. There are very few places where drug and alcohol addiction is cool, where entering rehab is a just another press release and not a solution to a very serious problem. In Hollywood, on any given night, someone like River Phoenix can stumble out of your club and die right there on the infamous Sunset Strip. Just steps away, at the Hotel Marmont, is where John Belushi overdosed and died. This is most certainly the land of excess, in which I am a participant. My only wish for those who seek this lifestyle is that they enter this place knowing all it holds, both good and bad. I wish all young people with stars in their eyes—women especially—heeded the examples of those who have gone before them. You must move through this concrete jungle with care and purpose.

By the end of the night, I was exhausted, but more than that, I was happy and secure in the knowledge that my years of being a user are over. I looked forward to going home with The Boy Toy and nestling into his arms and chest and thanking God that I am living a safe and healthy lifestyle. The Boy Toy's studio apartment was comfortable and womblike, and he did his very best to make me feel at home. In truth, however, being intimate with him was strange for me. I was uncomfortable with him sexually because I did not respect him. He has done nothing that I admire or want to know more about. Our conversations were shallow, and his life had very little substance. Although this works when we're in a crowded, noisy nightclub, during the more intimate, quiet times, it is awkward.

He was extremely passionate, however, and was certainly a thoughtful lover. He would stare at me with his piercing hazel eyes and kiss me softly from head to toe and was slow and easy inside me, yet, I was hardly aroused, because our lives are so different. There was no way I could feel connected, and if my mind can't feel it, my body certainly won't. I find it difficult to sleep through the night and into the morning and find myself leaving at around six. By seven the next morning, I am at home, relieving my nanny, getting my son ready for school, and dropping him off by eight fifteen. Something tells me this won't go on much longer, as its allure quickly wanes.

After just three months of wild nights out and a few cozy nights in, I'd had enough of The Boy Toy's club mentality. All of a sudden, the charming allure of his studio apartment in Hollywood and his late-model Jeep Cherokee began to translate into inadequacy. After all, this is the man who, when we first met, told me he was twenty-nine but later admitted he's really thirty-two.

What was I doing with this guy? I want friends who are focused and accomplished, friends who have goals and ambitions; not club hoppers who sleep all day and party all night. The Boy Toy was nothing more than a hanger-on, and the charm of his lifestyle had worn off. I see groups of people anxious to be famous, emulating what they think famous people do: drugs and drinking, late nights, and sleep-filled days. And it's true, that celebrity scene exists—sometimes in excess. But many stars have families, homes, and plans for the rest of their lives. They have wills, investments, insurance, and equity, as do I. Why would I carry on with a man who conducts his life so differently from the way I conduct my own? I want to be inspired and in the presence of those more accomplished and wiser than I.

Long story short, The Boy Toy is out, and so is anyone else who lives his or her life on a different level than I do. I love to dance and drink and be crazy and have sex. But I also want to learn and be witty and be around people who challenge my thinking. On making this decision, I sent Mr. Toy an e-mail on MySpace, which read, "I am leaving. Thanks for the ride." And with that, I signed off MySpace and out of his life.

CHAPTER TWENTY

Jesus Loves Me

n December 2006 I was scheduled to speak at a large evangelical church in the south. In the weeks leading up to the event, I became better acquainted with the church's pastor through a series of phone conversations and e-mails. Originally the purpose of these calls was to reassure him that I was the person he wanted to speak to his congregation.

It is very rare that I feel insecure or inadequate, but I must admit that the prospect of this speaking engagement made me a bit apprehensive. Just the thought of standing up to speak in front of a congregation of Holy Rollers was unnerving. What must they think of me, the crowned harlot destined for hell? I'm not exactly an avid churchgoer or fan of organized religion, even though I am fully aware of the power God has over my life, and the advantages to heeding his warnings and serving his Word. That said, I am far from righteous. I am, in fact, very uncomfortable in houses of worship, at least during organized services. I want solitude when I talk to God. I prefer to pray in empty churches, and do so at my neighborhood chapel, St. Francis de Sales.

As the pastor and I continued our conversations, I began to feel more comfortable with the idea. I even looked forward to it and wondered how the experience would change me. I am obviously a work in progress. I have been going through a wondrous transformation over the past few years of my life. Each day I feel changed by my experiences and the revelations as life unfolds. At the age of twenty-eight, I feel I have begun to put my lewd and scandalous past behind me, and look forward to the changes that are to come. I feel no need to rush, however. I would like to take my time on my journey and feel every bump in the road.

As I prepared to make the trek down south, I began to think of what I would say to a couple thousand Christians, and to consider what they might say to me. I was drawing a blank, but since the pastor invited me to be part of an entire weekend he was calling the Honesty Experience, I figured I was in good shape. As my first book proved, I always tell the truth, sometimes to a fault, even when it's not what you want to hear.

One day shortly before I was to leave, the pastor called me with a stern tone in his voice. "I need to chat with you," he said somberly. "I was on your Web site last night and found some things that disturbed me. I am not promoting sin," he declared.

Now, to backtrack a bit, the Honesty Experience was billed as a forum in which to discuss the ills and pitfalls of the hip-hop culture and its music. Naturally, when one thinks of ills and pitfalls as it pertains to the hip-hop world, my name might be likely to come up. I have come to expect this, and actually enjoy bringing the unknowing public up to speed on what that life is really like. But what was the pastor talking about when he mentioned not wanting to promote sin?

I was perplexed because he had pictures of Jay-Z, Kanye West, Diddy, and 50 Cent, none of whom were scheduled to attend the conference, printed on the flyers used to promote the event, along with a photo of me taken from the cover of *Smooth* magazine. My question to him then became, which one of us being used to promote this little church is not a sinner or has not promoted sin in either our past or present works? Look at the company I'm in! What am I, the only sinful one in the bunch? The pastor went on to explain that it was a video journal entry on my Web site that got his boxers all in a bunch. In the "decadent" video in question, I was sitting in my Jacuzzi, up to my collarbone in suds, wishing everyone a happy Thanksgiving.

You can still see the turkey day video on my Web site, www.karrine.com. The only exposed skin is on my face, arms, and shoulders. Now, keep in mind that this is the same man who divulged to me that he loves *King* magazine and the "fine ladies" on display in every issue, the same man who told me that just nights before, he had been at a nightclub having a drink and meeting with a young lady who had flown in from Atlanta to visit him, the same pastor who couldn't stop telling me how "fine" I am, and the very same pastor who took an oath before God and witnesses when he married, then found himself divorced.

Okay, I see—you enjoy the blatant display of black ass on the pages of a national magazine, see no problem having sex outside wedlock, secretly visit nightclubs, consume alcoholic beverages, and deface the sanctity of marriage, but a woman in her bathtub, showing no skin below her armpits, is offensive to you? Got it.

The pastor then went on to explain that he somehow had found a full-frontal nudity photo of me online showing, as he so gracefully put it, "pubic hairs," while in a bathtub. My retort was simple: "I am sorry to disappoint you, Pastor, but I have never taken such a photo." But even if I had, why would that bother this man of God, a man who was already fully aware of my past? He knew about the distasteful moniker Superhead, which I have come to loathe with every fiber of my being, and *still* called on me to speak to his congregation. After my fact checkers combed the Internet and found no such photo, I started to wonder what his problem could be.

Maybe it was the fact that the pastor had taken it upon himself to book a coach ticket for me to fly into his town, and when he was made to change it to a first-class flight, he opted to use my frequent-flyer miles to upgrade the ticket for a mere hundred-dollar fee—without my consent! When I found out about the thirty thousand miles missing from my frequent-flyer account, American Airlines informed me that the chunk of mileage was equivalent to one thousand eight hundred dollars. Coincidently, the day before, my attorney notified the pastor that he would have to pay either the difference between the coach and first-class fare or the amount it cost to replace the miles he used. All of a sudden, I became a super sinner.

The fact was that the pastor underestimated how much my time and energy were worth, and either could not or would not pay more than the three hundred fifty dollars he splurged for his Honesty Experience weekend. Honesty Experience indeed! Instead of being honest with me, as I had been with him—and with the rest of the world, for that matter—he decided to blame it all on a bubble bath and a full-frontal nude photo that never existed. In the interim, the pastor also deemed it necessary to ask me if I had "accepted Jesus Christ as my personal Lord and Savior."

Oh, boy, here we go. Another dose of the double standard, just as with Tyra Banks and Donnie Deutsch. No, I told him, I had not given my life to the Lord, and if I had, I'd be celibate until marriage. I would no longer consume alcohol or smoke the occasional cigarette, nor would I continue to write books that are not directly related to God Himself. "I am not saved," I told the pastor as he stood sanctimonious and tall on his judgmental soapbox. "I am not saved, nor do I want to be. I am not a follower of any particular denomination and am, most certainly, not a follower of pastors who are so eloquent in their ways of quoting scripture yet do not live holy lives."

I admit it, I was on a roll, and I went on letting him have it.

"Which begs the question," I continued, "which of us are living holy lives? In my opinion, the day any one of us becomes so holy that we hold ourselves above the rest who inhabit the earth, and believe we are justified in our judgments of other men and women, that is the day the Lord will call us home to serve next to Him."

In the aftermath of my tirade, I felt drained but incredibly serene. I saw how someone who professes to be a high servant of God had plugged the holes of his insecurity by turning on me and questioning my lifestyle choices, picking on something as simple as a bubble bath. By trying to degrade me, he was able to deflect scrutiny of his own shortcomings—and do so in the name of the Lord. I told him, as I have told many, that when people reach a place in their lives where they are truly happy and blessed, and know they are adequate within their own lives, it becomes impossible for them to judge others or to turn even the most troubled soul away. Everyone is capable of projecting his or her baggage onto you, even one who claims to live his life for God. This pastor had a chance to change my mind, and he missed it, but what I know for sure is that everything has its purpose, and there is a reason why my disaffection from organized religion remains to this day.

My ordeal with the pastor brought home something I have always known. We are all people trying to find our way, and even though there are books to guide us, books that, we are certain, have all the answers, we still have questions. Even a man of God will never truly be saved until he is in the arms of the Lord. Until that day, he will always be affected by the world around him. That's what makes him a man, and that's what separates him from God Himself. The pastor and I would later smooth over our differences and continue our conversations, learning together. He would later admit his shortcomings and ask for forgiveness. For me, there was no foul to forgive. I can never fault a man for being flesh and bone, no matter how much that man may fault me.

CHAPTER TWENTY-ONE

Insomniac

There are nights when I cannot sleep, when my internal clock seems to stop. During the winter months, especially as the holidays near, I find myself eating more and falling asleep early in the evening, around seven thirty, and awaking around midnight. I lie awake until five most nights, battling feelings of anxiety. I wonder how long I will enjoy this ride, and if my life is really as great as I think it is. There are nights when I am no longer sure about who I am or what I'm doing here. I doubt myself on these nights and long for the security I found in Bill's arms.

He and I broke up in January 2006, and it was one of the most painfully necessary moments in my life. From the night we met in April 2005, I knew he was the one for me and that I would love him all the remaining days of my life. Our relationship was as close to perfect as one could have. He did all he could to please me, but I was ungrateful. Our differences in age and culture never seemed to matter until I realized how poorly trained and inexperienced I was in the art of relationships. I will always safeguard our love, for it still exists, and after a difficult split and harsh feelings, we have managed to stay close and have become closer in ways we never were before. He is the love of my life, and I know that no matter where we are or who we're with, our hearts are joined.

But it's nights like these, when the world is quiet and I am left alone with my thoughts, that I regret most that we are no longer together. I long for his arms around me and those kisses he gave me every night before bed. I miss having my clothes in his closet, my car in his driveway, my toothbrush next to his. We are better now than we have been, and I wouldn't change the way our relationship ended and started again—but still I mourn, especially on nights like this, when sleeping is impossible.

As I wait for morning, I think about *Confessions* and what it has done to my life, and ask myself if I would do it all again. Sometimes I regret the book that changed my life. I wonder what it is about me that allows me to be so brazen, so blunt, and to do things so many would never think of or would be embarrassed to try. When I lie awake, I beat myself up about the decision to start something I'm not sure I can finish. Am I really a writer, though I have written since the age of five? Am I really good at this, or did I just get lucky? What if I fail? It scares me to death to think that after all this I could very well fall flat on my face and hear the rest of the world laughing at me, saying, "I told you so." I feel as if I am changing at an impossible speed, and as I try to take the rest of the world along with me, I fear they will neither understand nor want me to change. Can I give the world my life without selling my soul?

As dawn comes and the day struggles out of darkness, I wonder if I have been a good mother. I worry that my nomadic ways are brushing off on my son, and whether that can be a good thing. My circle of intimate friends is small by design, but my friends all seem to have hundreds of their own friends. They're out and about while I'm at home alone, working during the day and asleep well before nine at night, except for the nights when I give myself room to breathe and enjoy Los Angeles's night life. I stay in my room during the evenings and rarely give the other rooms in my home any wear. My son does the same thing, and when I invite him to leave his bedroom he'd rather stay in and play his video games and DVDs and with his action figures. He has play dates several times a week and lets loose with his friends, although, according to their parents, the other kids prefer their bedrooms as well.

I sometimes feel strange for not wanting more friends and for having the ability to go out alone, treating myself to lunch or drinks. But as I lie awake in bed, envying my friends, I also compare us and find another important difference: I have more responsibilities in life than they and am significantly more successful than any of them. Maybe my mother was right when she taught us girls that we don't need friends and should learn to be alone. It has its advantages, I guess. But there are days and nights when I am lonely, wishing I had the life some of my friends do, just as there are days and nights in which I am happy I don't. I drive myself crazy at night wondering why, questioning my life and feeling guilty for doing so. By morning, however, it all seems to go away, and with the dawn's first rays of sunshine I am a confident and secure person with her entire life in order. But which one is the real me? And who says just one of them has to be? There's so much I don't know about life, love, and myself. Learning is painful, and mistakes are inevitable, but the one thing I know for sure is that at the end of it all, I'll never forget these days or these long, sleepless nights.

I am often asked if I harbor any regrets, and indeed I do. I feel guilty for those regrets because I hate to question God's work and wonder if I have done the right things, no matter how wrong they were. Every step of my life has gotten me to where I am today, and though it's not the perfect life, whose is? And the nights when I sit up, unable to sleep, wondering these things, I remind myself of a quote credited to Socrates: "The unexamined life is not worth living." As annoying as it is not to have all the answers, I know I am doing the right thing by questioning. There was a time in my life when I never questioned myself, when I just assumed I was doing the right thing because I was doing what I wanted to do. Now I think long and hard before making decisions, and once the decisions are made I contemplate their consequences. I make mistakes every day of my life, but that's okay because I will never make the same mistake twice, and I will never be the same person twice. I will always be better than I was the day before. And that I can never regret, nor will it keep me up nights.

CHAPTER TWENTY-TWO

Bored to Death with Life

As the rest of the country and most of the world prepares for Christmas and the New Year, I am left with the uncontrollable and sometimes laughable feeling of sheer boredom. The irony of it is all too painful as I look around at my life filled with a beautiful son, thriving career, safe and warm home, and the ability to do almost anything I want in life. My opportunities are boundless, and though I am grateful and extremely humbled by my recent success, I am simultaneously incredibly bored with my life, socially.

This is the time of year when I like to do a bit of housecleaning, and not the type that requires soap and water. This type requires a change of phone number, e-mail address, atmosphere, and friends. As I scroll through my electronic Rolodex, I am overcome by how many people in it are not intellectually stimulating. Although I know many interesting, charming, and funny individuals, very few of my closest friends are able to add to my life in ways I crave most. I am eager to learn and discover new things; for instance, I have gained an insatiable interest in the theater and opera as well as in current events, nationally and abroad.

My friends who are closest to my age lead entirely different lives, with less responsibility and ambition. They seem to think of themselves as children still—as if we were to live out our twenties as an extension of our adolescence. My belief, on the other hand, has always been that at the age of twenty-five, all excuses end; after twenty-five you basically go right to thirty. Once I came upon that milestone birthday, I began to put my first five-year plan into action, and just a few years later I have witnessed what a bit of creativity, brazenness, and ambition will accomplish. But then again, most of my girlfriends aren't mothers, either, and that accounts for the majority of my drive.

Everyone is different, I know that, and all my friends bring their own unique qualities to my life and enrich it in their very own special ways. Still, I need more. There is so much to be said for success and the freedom it brings. It's the ability to fall asleep at night without worrying about what the next day will bring; to know that the bills are paid. I remember all too well the stress of watching bills come in. They would sit on my kitchen counter for months, going unpaid because there was nothing to pay them with. I no longer see the bills—they go straight to my accountant, and that's very liberating. What success has done for me is to give me the luxury to enjoy life and to indulge my thirst for exploring it. Not all my friends are able to this, and the ones who are, the famous and wealthy ones, sometimes bore me as well. Not to mention that most people in the entertainment industry are too self-centered to travel outside their own intellectual comfort zone, and those who are more well rounded are significantly older than I and are good only for those deep, meaningful conversations. The problem with that is that sometimes I just want to party or pick up at the last minute and drive to Palm Springs for the weekend to enjoy a hot springs mud bath. My older friends aren't so adventurous—if you can consider Palm Springs adventurous!

I wish I could have all these different qualities in someone other than Bill. Smart and funny, accomplished and comfortable— someone who is driven yet takes time to enjoy life. Not to say that Bill isn't enough, but he shouldn't have to be. I would like to sit in a circle of my peers and talk about career and life choices, mortgage rates, and property taxes. I would love to engage in debates about the writings of Chekhov and Gibran, and sometimes I just want to talk about nothing at all. I guess I simply want the option—I want it all, it seems, and this most likely falls under the context of dreaming the impossible dream. Whatever the circumstances or context, I am bored and look forward to meeting new people as I and my life evolve.

As the New Year approaches, I am looking forward to a new start and very necessary endings, which is the only way I know how to grow up and outward and to remain enthusiastic about life.

My New Year's resolution for the year 2007 was simple: to be happy, to be healthy, and to live life as though I mean it. Little did I know that waiting around the corner for me was the man who would change everything—again.

CHAPTER TWENTY-THREE

Auld Lang Syne

he year 2007 worked itself into my life with little fan-
fare, if any. As the clock struck twelve, I was sound
asleep in my bed, comfortable and confident that the
past year had come and gone just the way it ought to. It may have
started with the most devastating breakup of my life, but it ended
serenely with me surrounded by all my accomplishments—and the
most important of these is the happiness and security I have supplied for my young son. As he lay asleep in his bed, unaware of the
festivities outside, I couldn't imagine a better person to ring in the
New Year with.

Under all this peace and joy, however, anxiety burned in the pit of
my stomach. Unlike last year's this anxiety was of the healthy variety.
Several weeks earlier, I had met a boxer named Antonio Tarver, and
he had managed to sneak his way into my heart, no matter how hard
I tried to keep him out. At first, everything about him seemed the
opposite of what I want in my life. He's big and boisterous, with a boyish smile and an uproarious laugh. He's a professional athlete, which,
as a rule, I steer clear of, based on past dating experiences with NFL,
NBA, and other boxing professionals. Between their arduous travel

schedules, the women they tend to collect around the world while on the road, and their strip club off-season antics, being the lover, girlfriend, or wife of a professional athlete isn't all it appears to be.

So when this tall, dark man jumped from a moving car to give me his phone number while I stood waiting for the valet at the Four Seasons Hotel to bring me my vehicle, I reluctantly pressed the digits into my phone, pretending to save it. He seemed very anxious and not as confident as he might be when meeting women. When I introduced myself, he told me he already knew who I was, and that's when the doubts filled my head. Was I to believe that he wanted to get to know me so we could have intellectual conversations over tea and scones? Or should I just admit the truth: when a man walks up to a woman on the street with the desire to court her, he is doing so based solely on physical appearance and sexual drive. Once a man gets to know her, then he may become attracted to her sense of humor, her ability to engage in intellectual banter, and the way she carries herself in the presence of friends and family. To get to that point takes time, but before that, each person in the relationship has to give the other a chance, which is something I was not interested in doing.

As Antonio walked away with an aura of accomplishment, I smirked, knowing he would never hear from me again. I slid into my car, opened the hardtop, and cruised home, never to think of him again—that is, not until the following day. True to my usual routine, I found myself back at the Four Seasons, writing on my laptop in the same corner of the lounge I frequent daily with a glass of the establishment's finest cabernet sauvignon to accompany my flank steak and mashed sweet potatoes. As I sat there alone, I wondered about the hotel's boisterous guest who risked life and limb jumping out of a moving vehicle to capture my attention. Was he in the building? Could I be so close to him and not, at least, find out what I'd be missing if I continued to ignore him completely? Though I didn't save his phone number in my phone, oddly enough, it was stored in my newly acquired photographic memory, which I must have picked up the moment he gave me his number. Reluctant but curious, I decided to call.

His deep voice and Southern drawl was comforting to my ear as he answered the phone. "Hello?"

"Hey, it's Karrine."

"Oh, hey!"

"Look, just wanted to let you know I'm back at the Four and you can join me while I work and eat, if you'd like."

"Well, I'm out having breakfast right now, but I'm going to finish up here and come right to you."

"That's fine." I tried to remain stern and unaffected by him, but there was something exciting and a bit frightening about meeting him. As a rule, I very rarely allow new people into my life. I live in a social cocoon where everything and everyone is the same all the time. I feel safer this way, and my chances of being hurt are greatly minimized by my routine. In the event that I do decide to let some-one new into my life, I make a predetermined date by which that person will have to go. As with The Boy Toy, in my heart I knew I couldn't carry him into my New Year. This time of year is for more permanent people, and with his wild, late-night ways, I knew he'd only last only a season. I have a life full of rules and restrictions for myself and for those around me, and though they are in place for my own good, the effects of these rules aren't always in my best interest. I know that I am missing a lot of life because I am afraid of being hurt and disappointed again. As much as I attest to what a brave woman I am, inside I am still a very scared little girl who is, in many ways, broken and trying very desperately to heal.

During this healing process, another wound would be badly damaging, and I find myself protecting my heart with vigor and valor, stubbornness and stupidity. I know that with such armor around my heart I could very well miss out on someone wonderful. And for the past year, I have decided that's okay. I have decided to do without, which means that Antonio cannot become a part of my life—absolutely, unequivocally, no.

Antonio made his way to my table at the Four Seasons, sat down, and started asking questions, some personal, some professional, in an attempt to know me better. I was reluctant to answer any of his inquiries, reluctant to let him in, if even just a little bit. But there was something about his eyes and face that soothed me. There was a boyish charm behind this man nearly in his forties. His eyes danced and his smile seemed sincere and pure. Once we started talking, I was surprised to find how natural the conversation was, as well as stimulating to all my senses. I liked his way of dress, the way he swaggered into the room, his cologne. Everything about Antonio was so enticing that I found myself drawn to him, even though I tried hard not to show it.

After my lunch, Antonio escorted me to the mall after insisting that he needed a new pair of sneakers for his workout. The ride to the Beverly Center was short, and we found ourselves strolling through Macy's Men's Store, then into the elevator. Within his first hour of meeting me, he was met with one of my phobias. Because I am claustrophobic, I have a difficult time in elevators, especially those in malls and parking structures. Many times I will go out of my way to find an escalator or the stairs in order to reach my destination without having an anxiety attack. And as with most things in my life, there is a rule to the phobia. If I absolutely have to get into an elevator, I prefer to ride in one with just a few people in it. Even then, I am counting the seconds until I can escape.

Antonio found my affliction strange, but from the moment we stepped into the elevator he tried to ease my silly phobia by taking me into his arms, burying my head in his chest, rubbing my back, and telling me it would all be okay. Though the ride was short, this feeling of intimacy stayed with me, and I fought it all the way. He seemed so forward as he tried to hold my hand while making our way through the mall. I pushed him away when he tried to kiss my face, and shot down all his other advances. I didn't want to let him in, at least not then. The truth was, however, that I knew I would, but I was determined to make him work harder than he had ever worked for anything in his life.

I dropped him off at the Four Seasons, promising to see him later that evening. I was outwardly unaffected, but on the inside my thoughts danced with the unknown. Who was Antonio, and how would he fit in my life? Was I really breaking my own rules and agreeing to let him in?

There are so many things I do not know, by head or by heart, and I am eager to learn. Many times learning means taking chances, and I was about to make a new rule for the New Year: enjoy my life without fear; know that everything happens for a reason; and nothing is allowed without God's will. The worst days of my life are over, and I have grown enough to know how to protect my heart.

Often I think of my mother, and I am reminded of what I do not want to be. I don't want to go through my life telling everyone how much I don't need them, that I am all right being by myself. The truth is, everyone needs someone sometime, and independence can easily turn into loneliness and regret. Unlike my mother, I refuse to enter my middle age alone, looking back and wondering what could have been. There is a thin line between good old-fashioned courting and pushing a good man away. There is a dance to be had, but even in a vigorous tango there is give and take and, finally, submission. I realized that I was fighting visions of old ghosts that only existed in my mind. If I believe that *Confessions* was my purging, I truly have to let it all go, give it all back to the universe and stop using it as an excuse.

For the past year, I had used Bill as an excuse not to move on.

And though, since the moment we met and fell in love, I have always been sure that he is the one I want to spend the rest of my life with, I have been able to care for others while Bill and I regroup and return to the core of our relationship. Antonio, in a very short time, seemed to become a wonderful part of my life, and Bill seemed like just a memory. Antonio had to leave Los Angeles just a few days after we met, and headed back to his hometown of Tampa, Florida.

After that he called me several times a day, and we'd talk for hours on end. I was still fighting my impulses, and he was still trying to conquer these walls around my heart. He was kind, and I was brutal. I would start fights over the most mundane things: Why didn't you call me back? Why are you always out with your friends? Why would you take some girl to the movies? None of this mattered, but it was self-sabotage. If I could make him hate me, he would go away—that was my intent, but finding a way to make him back off would prove impossible. Every time I would fight and try to wiggle my way out of his emotional hold, he would respond with kindness and understanding, with patience and love. I couldn't stand it!

He was winning the war, and all my antics wouldn't scare him away. He was the first person I spoke to in the morning, and the last voice I would hear at night. He filled my days with witty banter and laughter. I looked forward to his calls and was sure never to miss one. His name went from Antonio to "baby," and he returned the gesture. This stranger was becoming comfortable, and soon we made plans to meet again, at six in the morning in Tampa, on January 2, 2007. I would begin my New Year with him, in his home, with my son. This trip was more than a visit with a lover—it was my future and my past coming together. It was my life coming full circle, as the new me touched down in this old place where my life had gone from bad to worse. This is where I came when, at the age of ten, my mother moved us from St. Thomas to a small suburb of Tampa.

At a time in my life when everything was brand-new, it was

strange to think of going back to this place for the first time in thirteen years. I imagined what it would be like to go back to the apartment complex my mother and I moved into when we first arrived in Tampa during the winter freeze of 1987. This is the place I went home to after being kidnapped and raped at the age of thirteen, and I was beaten by my mother as I stepped through the doorway. In this same place I sat and looked out the window at the playground, listening to Patti LaBelle's "Somebody Loves You" and wondering who that someone was, knowing I'd never be a child again.

This was the same place where I spent a lonely Christmas in my room with no gifts under the tree, listening to my sisters tear away at theirs. In a strange twist of fate, my mother had recently just moved back to that same apartment complex. She was moving backward, and I, in the opposite direction. Here we were, right back where we started, except that one of us was very, very different. This is where my son would play as he visited his grandmother, unaware of the pain that still resides within those walls for his mother. He was looking forward to going, and I was dreading the trip.

This vacation would be my son's first airplane ride since he was a year old and too young to remember. No matter what happened, it was up to me to remain calm despite what I may feel about my past life in Tampa. To see the look on his face as the plane took off from Los Angeles International, I was so very happy that he was so excited. I felt like a good mother, and the look on his face assured me that to him, I was doing the right thing. He was allowed inside the cockpit once the plane landed, where we took photos of him in the pilot's seat.

Between his first airplane ride and my jitters about being alone with Antonio, Naiim and I were both vibrating with excitement when we stepped off the plane in Tampa. Antonio was waiting when we arrived, just as tall, just as dark, and just as handsome as I remembered. All of a sudden, it was as if I'd known him for years. I felt at home as I walked toward him, and I knew I'd be safe—just as I had been when he comforted me in the elevator weeks before. I was going to take a chance on love again. I was going to let my guard down and give Antonio things that I hardly give to any man—respect, consideration, *and* the benefit of the doubt. Hell, I may even submit once in awhile. Put down my sword and give up the ghosts.

CHAPTER TWENTY-FOUR

Death of a Vixen

Visiting Tampa for the New Year held a lot of significance for me, as my past and my present collided. I was forced to make important decisions about my future. There was a new man in my life, and though neither of us knew how far this relationship might go, what was clear to me is that if I ever wanted a relationship with a man to work on any level, there were habits I must leave behind. Not every disagreement merits a fight. Some things in life are actually easy, if you let them be.

For the first time since Bill, I was going to allow a man to love me—to care how my day has gone, to administer medicine when I am ill, and to feed me from his plate when I am hungry. These are gestures that may seem small to people who have always had them, but there had been only one man in my life who cared for me so completely. Now, for the first time since the day Bill and I met, someone else had shown me thoughtfulness, kindness, and love. And I must allow him to love me.

Antonio managed to become the yin to my yang. When I would fight with him, he would fight me back, but not with force. He would fight with such compassion and understanding that I would have no choice but to stop the fight. It's the same fight my mother has fought all these years. I come from a long line of confused women who spend their nights alone or wondering what could have been, women who have fought their way to nowhere and for a cause they have never known.

I cannot fight against kindness anymore. I listen to Mother speak, and I can hear the bitterness and the delusional sense of entitlement. As she so proudly puts it, she has "mastered the art of separation," a skill I am not interested in learning. I have no wish to be known as someone who is an expert at running men out of her life. I do not wish to put that energy into the universe and have it return to me as prophecy. What I know for sure now is that I don't need someone else to live, but I do need someone to love.

In that regard I'm like everyone else. My heart breaks, and there are times in my life when I find myself crying more than I smile. The point of this relationship with Antonio is not to fall in love and live happily ever after, but to teach myself how to allow someone to love me. And with my hardened heart, to continue to learn how to love in return. When I use this word "love," I do not do so in a romantic context; I use it in its truest and deepest meaning.

As my new life met with the memories of my past in Tampa, I was also forced to consider whether to revisit the place where it all started, the first place my family landed when we moved from St. Thomas to the United States—the place where my life went from bad to worse. At first, I felt an obligation to go back to that apartment complex and face my demons. I felt as if I had to stare my past in the eye and show it that I had moved on. But then I asked myself, *If I have truly moved on, why go back there? What do I have to prove—and to whom?* I don't have to do anything to prove that I have moved on—except to keep moving on. I chose not to go. My sister drove out to Antonio's home to pick up my son and take him to visit his grandmother for a couple of days.

While writing this book, I have been very mindful of all the women I have met who praised me for penning *Confessions of a Video Vixen*. From celebrities like Jane Fonda to the everyday woman, I have received love and admiration for my ability to be honest in the face of judgment. At first I didn't know what to do with this responsibility or even if I should have it at all. As I sat down to complete *The Vixen Diaries*, I wanted to do each of these women justice.

My life has come full circle, and I will no longer be defined by who I was in the past. I will not hide from pain or happiness, and I will never be what others may think of me or want me to be. Most recently I have managed to make small yet significant changes that have only improved my quality of life. I will no longer beat myself up about mistakes. I will always make them, but the key is to make different, better mistakes and follow them up with smarter resolutions. The days of *Confessions* are far behind me, and I will never again allow them to be the biggest part of me. Those days were only the beginning of my life, and no matter how hard some may try, that book and those days will never fully define me. I am so much more than I have given myself credit for in the past, and I deserve the very best of everything, as does everyone. Now I am determined to have it.

As I sat in Antonio's bed in Tampa, my laptop warming my thighs and the clicking of its keys resounding throughout the room, I could feel how different I was from where I started. Not just where I started in that city, but different from each new start I ever had. Before this time in my life, I never knew what the term "growing pains" meant. As a child I would think, *I grow every day, but I don't feel a thing.* I couldn't say the same now, not even in jest. I feel every moment of every day of my life, and some days this growing hurts like nothing I have ever known. Even in the pain, however, I take some comfort. Because of it, I know that I am changing and will never be the same person twice. Thank God for that.

I was leaving Tampa with the loose ends of my girlhood tied

together and with a clearer understanding of the sort of person I *don't* want to be. Many times as we grow older, we find ourselves becoming just like our parents, no matter how far the distance or time between us. I find it amazing how my son does things his father used to, though they have never known each other. . . . things like running his fingers up and down his arms while he sleeps and demanding to eat only waffles for breakfast most mornings. And even though I have been thousands of miles away from my mother for over thirteen years, there are things about me that are a direct result of her habits and behaviors. These were ideas put into my head as a child, over time. I find myself repeating these ideas out loud and perpetuating a cycle of stupidity. I cannot blame it all on my mother, since I also find myself doing and saying things the same as my father. Neither is becoming.

As I look at the relationship between my mother and all three of her daughters, I am sure she must be filled with regrets and what-ifs. It seems that all of us are doing something in our lives that our mother never did or had the opportunity to do. I am a financially secure homeowner; my first sister is a hardworking full-time student in a long-term relationship; and my second sister holds down a lucrative job and only accepts the best. Not yet twenty-one, she finds herself making more money than our mother ever made. Each of us is constantly wanting and achieving more. In a way, that is the goal of parenting: to watch your children grow up to have a better life than you did. On the other hand, however, it is sad when a parent is stunted by fear, pain, and embitterment.

My mother seemed unable to say one nice word about Antonio, me, or anything the two of us did together while I visited. When I told her we were headed to the golf course, where he lives in a planned community, her first comment was, "Oh, you don't have anything nice enough to wear to a golf course!" Bam! If I ever wondered what she thought about my taste in clothing, I was no longer in doubt. She then went on to tell me that because golf was invented in Scotland, I should tell Antonio that if he has never golfed there, "he's not doing anything." Bam again! As if living in a private resort on a golf course wasn't enough for her, he has to go to Scotland to tee off? What is wrong with this woman? When I told her which community we were in, her first comment was, "I don't like those homes. They are so close together." Yet another blast at someone who had never done anything to her! Well, Mom, you know what's close together? Apartments.

My mother tried her best to shoot down everything I said about Antonio and the time we were having together. She seemed determined to ruin my perception of this man and of my life in general. Never once was she supportive. Never once could she say, "Oh, that's nice." And as I listened to this shell of a woman, declaring how content she is with her life, yet spewing only venom and discontent, I wondered what brought her to this place and how I could avoid the same fate. This could be me in twenty years, I told myself, if I am not careful.

Did she feel let down when her father and mother split? Was it tough being the only legitimate child out of seven and being the prettiest, with the lightest complexion? Did she always have to fight to prove herself? Was she searching for love from early in her youth? And when our father left her with me, was she destroyed? And what about her next daughter's father, and the one after that? I was there, and I remember—they hurt her.

The list goes on and on after that, and just as I have found in my life, none of them stayed. When it's all said and done, you find yourself left with memories and battle scars, children, and shattered dreams and promises. Each man's job seems to be to fix the mistakes of the one before, each of them making up for a father who hurt you. It never ends, until you call it out and rip its roots from your core. And then you never go back there, to that place where it all started, where it all went wrong. That was my challenge and my goal. I know no other way to avoid the bitterness that comes with holding on to pain and disappointment and making everyone else pay for the mistakes made before them. If I live my life this way, I will never be happy—and that is just not an option.

I didn't mention any of this to my mother as she rattled on about all the things that are wrong with everyone else. I just held it inside. This is where I come from, and this is what I refuse to be. I know from experience that complaining about even the most obvious of her mistakes and shortcomings never ends civilly. Everyone is wrong, and she has all the answers. This is about the time when Dr. Phil would interject and ask, "So . . . how's that working for you?"

As I wrapped up my trip to Tampa and made plans to return in just two weeks and every two weeks after that, I left feeling hopeful and a bit afraid. Naturally, I looked forward to the year ahead, to going home to the life I have built over the past several years. But I wondered about my heart and its newfound vulnerability. A part of me was just waiting for Antonio to let me down, but the biggest part of me was willing to take that chance—to be brave, know, and follow my heart, and to take a chance on life and love again. Most important, I looked forward to allowing someone else to care for me, knowing that Bill doesn't have to be the only one. It should be okay to let someone else in. Gone were the days of going backward because it felt safe.

However, for all my enthusiasm and wishful thinking, there is nothing I can do if the man I trusted has lied to me. Almost two months into my relationship with Antonio, everything I thought we were building crumbled around me, and the person I thought he was went missing as the true nature of our relationship became evident. He and I made it a habit to speak to each other every day and never to go longer than two weeks without seeing each other. I was comfortable at his home and among his friends, and in that short time I thought I had become a part of his life.

We had an incredible sex life. I found myself in positions I could have never imagined. We had marathon sessions of passionate, skin-to-skin, mouth-to-mouth, sweat-soaked coitus. There was nothing between us we didn't share—except the fact that three weeks before he met me, he'd proposed to the woman he'd been seeing.

When I first asked him if he was dating anyone, Antonio said there was a girl in Las Vegas he saw once in a while. On my first trip to Tampa, just two weeks after we met, I took it upon myself to call this girl, wanting her to know I was with him. Antonio insisted on keeping me a secret from her, and since he wouldn't prove that their relationship was as insignificant as he claimed, I took matters into my hands and dialed her number. As he and I talked late one night, I placed the call and laid the phone down, allowing her to hear our conversation. That night, his relationship with her ended. Or so I was told.

For the next two months he paraded me around Tampa, arm in arm, and let the city know we were together. We behaved in every way like a couple. We took pictures with fans and went out together almost every night. I watched him train during the day and enjoyed extended talks with his trainer over dinner. I had the full run of his home and free use of his cars: two Bentleys and a Range Rover. I could come and go as I pleased, but I was always sure to be home when he got there. On some nights, we'd stay in and I'd cook dinner for him. We would watch boxing matches on television and take long showers together. With his rigorous training schedule, his muscles were tight and achy, and as any caring woman would, I massaged his naked body for hours at a time, bringing him comfort. And that's all I ever did for Antonio, bring him comfort—except for the two occasions I punched him in the mouth.

In 2006, I learned how to be alone and love it. I learned how to heal from heartache—how to pick up the pieces and move onward. I learned how much I love my son and what a pillar he is in my life—without him, I could not stand. I learned what real love means: loving someone not *despite* their flaws but *because* of them, being a friend in fair and tumultuous weather and allowing that friend to love you back. I've learned to be kinder to those who are kind to me and, most important, to be kinder to myself. And to top it all off, as I entered 2007, I learned to let go and accept the death of a vixen.

What stands in the place of that vixen is a woman, confident and thick-skinned, a woman who cannot be broken by heartache but instead is strengthened by conflict—or at least that's what I thought. This theory was new to me as the New Year began. With my relationship with Antonio blossoming, it was the perfect time to test it. That day came just a few days after Valentine's Day, when I received a phone call from the game-playing boxer.

"Antonio, what's up? What are you doing?"

"I'm about to get married, Karrine."

"Shut up, stupid. What the fuck are you talking about?"

"I'm serious. I'm about to get married."

I waited a few seconds, absorbing what he had said. What was I to reply to that? This was the man I'd spent the past couple of months with, cooking and cleaning, introducing him to my family and bragging about him to my friends. He had become acquainted with my son and worked his way well into my life. Now, suddenly, he would be gone forever. There was only one thing I could say: "Okay, babe. Just call me when you're finished getting married."

With that, I hung up the phone and waited for my breakdown to begin. I waited and waited, but to my surprise, the breakdown never came, not even after he sent a text message saying, "I'm sorry, I have to do this. I love her."

My response? "Absolutely. She deserves it."

I sat around my home for the next two days, thinking and waiting for what used to be the inevitable emotional crash and burn. Nothing. No moping, no depression. Nothing. I sat in awe of myself, in shock at my composure. It seemed as if everything I thought of myself was true: I would never again be destroyed by a man. Two days later, I decided to join the rest of the world and the city of Los Angeles in celebration of the Oscars. My first stop would be *Black Enterprise* magazine at the elegant Beverly Wilshire Hotel—the *Pretty Woman* hotel. Emerging from my car, my eyes were locked on the red carpet as I walked toward it and the paparazzi that lined it. In the center of it all was a tall, dark, and handsome man with his arms around a woman. It was Antonio and his new bride.

I continued to walk toward the carpet with my heart racing in my chest, hoping I could keep my cool. I held my head high and maintained my smile as I approached. Cameras flashed as the awaiting photographers called my name. There we were: my lover, his wife, and me—and the only person between us was none other than Ray J. Perfect. Even a Hollywood script couldn't have conjured this up, and I couldn't have imagined a more uncomfortable scenario.

Luckily for me, I work best under pressure, and none of the onlookers could read the tension in the air. Antonio's wife tapped her new husband's arm and pointed in my direction. As he turned and looked at me, his eyes opened wide. I could almost see his heart pounding in his chest as he quickly turned back around, trying to focus his attention on the flashbulbs ahead while consoling his wife by stroking the back of her head. I continued to smile as I stood shoulder to shoulder with my longtime lover, Ray J.

One of the photographers asked Ray and me, "Are you two together?"

We looked at each other and laughed, "Nah, not at all!"

"Well, you never know with you two." Isn't that the truth!

A part of me wanted to point to Antonio and say, "I'm not with him, either, but I was just a week ago."

And as Antonio and his wife kissed, I recalled his face and lips between my legs, licking and sucking my clit and asshole. I wondered how I tasted to her.

CHAPTER TWENTY-FIVE

Sweetest Taboo

I continued to work my way around the *Black Enterprise* party, stopping to chat with business moguls André Harrell and Russell Simmons. I sat down with André and Russell for a few minutes to rest my aching feet and catch up briefly with the man who planted the seeds for my first book. As the story goes, it was André who recommended I turn my life story into a book, and though I felt at the time that the idea was too big, every time I saw André he would say just three simple words: "Write the book." And that I did.

Whenever I see André, I never miss an opportunity to thank him for the advice, and this night was no different. He allowed me to feel confident in making the decision, which—though it would uncover topics that have been taboo for me and for many people in my demographic—would serve a greater purpose than either of us ever realized. André turned to Russell and said, "Hey, Russ, I gave this girl an idea and she ran with it!"

"Yeah, I know!" Russell replied, and he turned and looked at me and said, "I need to be in business with you!"

When a man as accomplished as Russell Simmons says something like that to someone like me, a woman who has built her future from the ground up while looking to people like Russell and André for direction, it means the world. At that moment, I felt accepted and accomplished, moved and motivated.

It is moments like this that make it easier for me to ignore naysayers, because the people who really matter to me, the movers and shakers and history makers, acknowledge, encourage, and have even created my success. To them, neither I nor my books are taboo; they are just good business and marketing sense. As I glided through the crowd of A-list celebrities and top businesspersons, stopping along the way to chat, exchange business cards, and take pictures, I knew that I belonged there. Funny, but all of a sudden, whatever had been going on between Antonio and me seemed far away.

It seemed as if Mr. and Mrs. Antonio Tarver walked around the room once and left. We crossed each other's paths just once, and we all acted as if we didn't know that for the past two months we had shared intimate lives. But now, as I watched Antonio and his wife walk past me, I was satisfied knowing that I was done with him. I wanted her to have him because I wanted better. The next day, I would have better.

The following evening, *Ebony* magazine held an event in honor of the Oscars and gave awards to Halle Berry, Janet Jackson, and Forest Whitaker, who were in attendance. I floated around the room, feeling free and alive again. With Antonio out of my life, there was nothing to worry about. The theme of the night and of my life was now, "Why cry over spilled milk when there's a cow in the backyard?" I was a new woman, eager to date for fun and not for lifetime companionship. The pressure was off, and I was ready to submit to the fact that I was not just all right but better alone. Just when I was becoming accustomed to this idea, I was introduced to *him*.

To protect our privacy and relationship, I will call him "Baby Boy." He is beautiful and tall, with a smile that would melt any girl's heart, but he is young, very young. As we were being introduced in the midst of a crowded room, eyes on us, I was afraid to look at him. He had an air about himself that I couldn't comprehend. For someone so young, he carried himself like an experienced man throughout the night, stopping to make flirtatious comments here and there, flashing his boyish smile, and burning a hole through my false disinterest. I was smitten, but just the thought of it was taboo enough to keep me at bay. I decided not to pursue the young flirt. But Baby Boy noticed me when I noticed him, and while I wasn't looking he asked a mutual friend of ours for my phone number. This young man had class and smarts—and by the end of the night, he had me.

After dancing around each other for the last two hours of the event, we left at close to the same time and got into our cars, never saying good-bye. On the way home, I anxiously checked my phone, anticipating his phone call and practicing what I would say to him. I particularly practiced the way I would remain calm at the sound of his voice and pretend not to know he'd gotten my phone number from our friend. I was fifteen minutes into my drive home, and just seconds from my house, when my phone rang and my caller ID showed an unfamiliar number. Baby Boy was on the line.

"Hello?" I answered as unenthusiastically as possible.

"Karrine, it's Baby Boy."

"Oh, hey. What's up?"

"This is my number, so make sure to save it in your phone."

"Yeah, okay, but how the hell did you get *my* number?"

"I have my ways. So anyway, you have my number now, so call me anytime." Baby Boy and I began our relationship quite innocently that night, which was no precursor to how passionate and incredibly fulfilling our union would become in the very near future. He and I kept in touch on the telephone over the next several weeks, despite our increasingly time-consuming work schedules and family responsibilities. We found it difficult to find time to see each other and vowed to take the very first chance we could, no matter how short our time together might be. That first chance came one night in late February 2007.

Baby Boy made his first trip to my home around ten in the evening, and as he strolled up the walkway and toward my front door, my heart pounded with both excitement and fear. Here was this beautiful young man with his entire life ahead of him, walking into the arms of a much older woman. We were living on the edge and we knew it. There was something exhilarating about sneaking around with Baby Boy. I had whispered on the phone over the past several weeks so the people around us wouldn't hear. Now he was tiptoeing into my home, being careful not to be seen by my neighbors. And though this isn't the first time I've been with a man younger than me—such as Ray J—the age difference between Baby Boy and me is much greater.

He wandered through my home and around the backyard, taking the grand tour. The last stop on the mini excursion was my bedroom, including its newly remodeled bathroom. Just as I was showing off my slate, glass-enclosed shower with double shower heads, Baby Boy grabbed me from behind, pulled my sweat pants down to my knees, bent me over, and, as he puts it, gave me the business. I melted with sensual pleasure. I was in shock and ecstasy while simultaneously feeling guilty, wanting more and wanting him to stop all at the same time. I disconnected my body from his for a moment and steered us toward my bed, confused.

"We can't do this," I halfheartedly protested.

"Yes, we can."

"No."

"Yes." He planted his lips on my mine, and his sweet kiss extinguished my fight as I lay on my back, inviting him to mount me, to make love to me, to make it impossible for me to do without him from this night forward.

Slow and sensual, he moved inside me. Then I rolled on top of him, surprised by his size, unwilling and unable to handle it all. Our eyes were locked and fixed on each other as we explored each other's bodies and needs; I felt him and he felt me, and then it was over. His work schedule didn't permit him to stay long, and no matter how badly we wanted to continue, we couldn't. But we made plans to save the rest for later. Once he left, I sat in my room, wrapped in my rumpled sheets, smelling his cologne on my skin and the scent of the love we made between my legs. The taste of his kiss lingered on my lips, and the memory of our first sexual encounter would remain fresh in my mind from that day forth. Baby Boy was mine now, as was the secret of our forbidden relationship.

Over the next several months, he and I would spend night after night together, making love, talking, laughing, and getting to know each other slowly. We often found ourselves on opposite sides of the country and even the world as our work and obligations took us in opposite directions. However, no matter where we are in the world, no matter the space and time between us, we always manage to reconnect and take our relationship one step further. Each encounter we have breaks down walls, as he finds himself doing things he's never done before, allowing himself to be sexually free and comfortable with me. Though I am completely enthralled with our relationship, in the back of my mind I am often aware of the sizable age difference between us, which is both a danger and a thrill. There is no doubt that I shiver with the excitement of sneaking around in the middle of the night, keeping our forbidden love a secret.

It's not just the age difference that makes our relationship so taboo, but we know that if his family, friends, and colleagues thought he was seeing me, the much experienced, controversial author, they would lock him up and throw away the key. I would be seen as a predator, lurking over the young, handsome luminary, and the rest of the world would condemn our relationship before it ever had a chance to develop. Baby Boy and I continue to sneak around, sharing each other whenever and wherever we can. Contrary to what most of the people interested in my life believe, my life is filled with hundreds of secrets, most of which I will never reveal. Baby Boy is one, and he just may be the sweetest taboo yet.

But my relationship with Baby Boy is not the only thing in my life that is forbidden. In fact, my entire lifestyle may be. After years outside the music industry, somehow I have found myself right back in. I spent many years of long nights in smoky studios and trips on the road in a tour bus, backstage at concerts and hotel rooms, state to state. There is something about this life that draws me to it when I am in search of myself. All of a sudden, quiet dinners at the Four Seasons and spa days just aren't enough anymore; I want to taste that hip-hop life again and live on the wild side a bit—but do it smarter than I had before.

There is a definite difference in me now, thirteen years after I started mingling in the inner circles of sports and entertainment. I am wiser and more seasoned. I know the game and what it takes to be respected. I know when to show up and when to leave. I know how to use my intellect and not my body. These days, I walk into a room as Karrine Steffans, mother, *New York Times* best-selling author, entrepreneur, and woman to be reckoned with. I walk in with my head held high and without my hand out; I need nothing from anyone.

Now, as I sit in the recording studio late into the night, it's for the music, the feeling that hip-hop gives me. Hip-hop understands me in a mystical way, the pain that I am in and the dreams that drive me. Its rhythm and baseline beat along with my heart and give me the tempo in which to move through life. Now, when I spend late nights in hotel rooms with friends in the industry, it's for the sanity of being around creative people who also feel different from the rest of the world. It's for the laughter, the memories that I enjoy, and those late nights at clubs and stumbling out of them in the early morning. This lifestyle offers me relief from my everyday existence and stimulates my senses. It strengthens my writing and introspection. And besides all that, it's just plain fun.

I told myself years ago that I would never set foot back into this world. But maybe it's such a part of who I am that I can never be completely free from it. What I am free from is the naïveté and neediness that led to the promiscuous, drug-induced lifestyle of my past. I made hip-hop taboo for myself, thinking initially that it was the lifestyle that brought me down. And even though it is treacherous terrain, I am better equipped now to travel through it and make it out on the other side, all right. Or so I hope.

CHAPTER TWENTY-SIX

Notes on a Scandal: A Letter to Papa

Dear Papa,

It's been over seven years since we first met, and a little while since we have spoken, and I have to say, I miss you. During our years together you saw me through tremendous changes and never left my side throughout it all. Even after all this time, I continue to long for those late nights in bed with you when we'd share our secrets and our hopes and dreams for each other. You were always my greatest supporter and, in my eyes, my best friend. No matter who came in or went out of my life, you were a constant. You were my soft place to land when it all turned to shit. You would pick me up, dust me off, and send me back into the world after each heartache, telling me along the way, "I'm not going anywhere." Finally, you did, but only because I asked you to go.

When I met Bill, I thought our relationship had to change. I knew it was time for me to find a love of my own and to leave our affair behind us. The only way I knew how to do it was simply to walk away and vow never to look back. But even though the concept behind my departure was valid, I should never have discounted you as a friend. I have needed you so many times since then; I needed you desperately to pick me up and dust me off as you always had. But by the time I turned around to look, I could no longer reach you, and I now fear you're gone for good.

I know that what we had is impossible for the world to understand: how another woman's husband could mean so much to me and how I could love a man who could never be mine.

But that was never the point with us, was it? We were friends who became lovers and who found it impossible to break that bond after your marriage. There would be months when we wouldn't see each other. But you were always still there, on the other end of the telephone, with your fingers still on the pulse of my life. I could always depend on you. You lifted me up in some of my weakest moments. You fed my son and me when everyone else turned their backs on us, and you stood up for me when others did not. We both know our affair was wrong by the terms of the outside world. It hurt those who love us the most, and I deeply regret that part. However, our love and our friendship is still too meaningful for me to forget or to let go.

Life after Confessions has been crazy, but through it all I've returned to memories of you telling me I would be successful one day, and remembered how much you wanted to see me happy. Well, one out of two isn't bad, I guess. As I grow older I begin to wonder if happiness is ever really attainable. I find myself utterly satisfied and having the time of my life, but hesitant to say that I am truly happy, for fear of complacency. There are many happy moments throughout my days, but your absence detracts from any happiness I may ever experience.

I lie awake some nights and wonder how you are. I wonder if you're happy and living well. I find myself driving past the houses and hotels you've resided in, thinking of the jokes and the long nights watching movies and playing video games. I pray for you and wish for nothing but good for you, as I know you do for me.

Many times I recall the night we both ended up on a red-eye flight out of Los Angeles. It had been four months since we'd broken up, and Bill and I were in love and so happy together. But there we were, sitting together in first class, knowing we could never truly be finished. I remember running my fingers over your hand, just wanting to touch you. You said you missed me, and as I returned the gesture I rested my head on your chest and cried silently. I cried for who I was before, knowing that woman was gone, and for the fear of the unknown, of who I would be without you.

That night played out like a movie as we exited from the plane side by side, knowing that no one would see us at five in the morning. Fate seemed to play into our hands as we discovered that your transportation had not arrived, which gave you an excuse to ride along with me. As we followed my driver to the waiting Town Car and were driven to my hotel, my heart beat with both exhilaration and doubt. Was I really ready to move on without you? Could I ever give someone else all of me with you in my life?

I called Bill to let him know I had arrived safely, and told him I'd be going right to bed on checking into my hotel room. A single tear escaped my eye and rolled slowly down my face as I lied to the man I was in love with, while holding the hand of the man I loved before him. We walked into the lobby separately, but into my room together. I remember you had hurt your back, and how disappointed I was that I had to go easy on you, how I wanted to tear you apart. I had missed you too much, and by fate, there we were, together again.

As the morning sun rose over New York City, we made love

for the very last time. It was slow and passionate; we moved as if we knew we would never be that way again. I didn't want it to end, but the guilt was killing me. With each long, slow stroke, I held my breath and tried to make time stand still. Our love-making lasted a wonderful long time, but not forever, the way I wanted it to last. I lay in bed, wrapped in its crisp white sheets, and watched as you dressed. You asked me if I was happy, and I said yes. I lied.

What happened that night ... well, it was pivotal and final. As you left me, I knew I had to go on without you. I was discovering so much about my life, letting go of old things and trying to hang on to the new. That night I was faced with my most powerful weakness and was disappointed in myself as I proved that no matter how Bill loved me, you could steal me away, if only for a night. I hated myself for that.

Several months later, I found myself at L'Ermitage Hotel, engaged in a meeting with agents, when I looked up to see you rushing through the lobby. I couldn't control myself as I yelled out, "Papa! Papa!" I don't know what came over me. It was an insane gesture, as everyone in the lobby turned and looked to see who Papa was. As you dashed into the elevator, I sat back feeling defeated. How could I have done that?

After that terrible, embarrassing mistake, I felt sure that you would never speak to me again. As I stood at the parking valet a few hours later, I was surprised and delighted when I saw you jogging out of the elevator, heading right toward me. As I looked up at you from the sidewalk, how I wished you would take me away from the pain I was in.

That moment I realized I had made a terrible mistake by letting you go completely. I needed you to hold me and tell me that everything was going to be all right, that I would get over Bill in due time and I would regain my focus as a writer and mom. I needed the encouragement for which I had come to love you, but it was far too dangerous for you to give me what I needed at that moment. Of necessity, Confessions had put a wedge between us. The whole world was watching, and at that precise moment, every eye in the hotel was on us.

Later that night, we argued—or at least pretended to argue. It was the only way we could communicate without falling back into our old ways . . . and back into bed. You didn't care who saw us, as people looked on in the hotel; you've never been ashamed of me, not even at the height of the Confessions controversy. Although you never wanted to be revealed as Papa, you didn't shield yourself that night. As you told me about the problems Confessions caused you and how much you wanted to be left out of the whole thing, I watched as your body contradicted your words.

That's when I knew how powerful our connection was and will always be. You smiled as you yelled, but your eyes told me what I'd always known. You care for me; you miss me; you know my heart and that my life and yours will always be joined by those years between us. I've kept your secrets and defended your lies to the world. I keep your name tattooed on my back, and your ways etched in my heart.

Remember us. Remember your friend and what we built together. Know that I miss you and the support you have offered me over the years. Thank you for all you have been and meant to me in my past and even in my present day. I have not forgotten anything we've ever said, anywhere we've ever been, or any of the many wonderful experiences we've had together. You are now and will forever be a part of my life, regardless of the space and time between us. I have loved you since I was thirteen, though I couldn't touch you until I was twenty-one, selflessly walking away at twenty-six.

Well, Papa, I'm twenty-nine now, and I have grown quite a bit since our days together. I am finally okay without you. Still, I often find myself looking at my phone when it rings, wondering if one day it'll be you, my Papa, my past, my Method Man.

With Love,
Karrine